Collins
English for Life

A2 Pre-intermediate

Reading

Anna Osborn

Collins

HarperCollins Publishers
77-85 Fulham Palace Road
Hammersmith
London W6 8JB

First edition 2013

Reprint 10 9 8 7 6 5 4 3 2 1 0

© HarperCollins Publishers 2013

ISBN 978-0-00-749774-4

Collins ® is a registered trademark
of HarperCollins Publishers Limited.

www.collinselt.com

A catalogue record for this book is available
from the British Library.

Typeset in India by Aptara

Printed in Italy by LEGO SpA, Lavis (Trento)

HarperCollins does not warrant that
www.collinselt.com or any other website mentioned
in this title will be provided uninterrupted, that
any website will be error free, that defects will
be corrected, or that the website or the server
that makes it available are free of viruses or
bugs. For full terms and conditions please refer
to the site terms provided on the website.

About the author

Following a degree in Modern Languages at Oxford specializing in literature, **Anna Osborn** worked in publishing as a Managing Editor during the 1990s. She retrained to become an English language teacher in 2000 and has since worked across Europe teaching students of all levels and ages. In addition, she has written a wide variety of English language learning materials including business and general study books, online self-study courses, and classroom workshops. Her most recent books were *English for Business: Speaking* (Collins, 2011), and *English for Life: Reading* (*B1*) (Collins, 2012).

CONTENTS

INTRODUCTION

Collins English for Life: Reading will help you to improve how you read by providing reading practice in real-life situations.

You can use *Reading*:
- as a self-study course
- as supplementary material on a general English course

Reading has 20 units, divided into four sections:
- Communication
- Around town
- On the move
- In your free time

Unit structure

The 20 units of *Reading* have a similar structure. Each unit begins with a 'Getting started' section with questions to get you thinking about the subject matter of the unit. Then each unit is divided into two or three sections, which include:
- reading texts that are typical of their type.
- detailed comprehension exercises to check that you have fully understood each text.
- practical reading activities to help you to practise reading in the best way for each particular type of text.
- language exercises before and after the text to help you to understand any difficult vocabulary and get the most out of each text.

Other features
- 'Reading tip' boxes include useful information to help you to improve your reading.
- 'Language note' boxes give extra information about the language in the texts.

At the back of the book there are some useful sections:
- **Appendix 1:** *How should I read?* explains the different kinds of reading skills you need to practise.

- **Appendix 2:** *Practical reading study tips* provides useful techniques to use when reading, for example taking notes or keeping a vocabulary notebook.

- **Appendix 3:** *Reading specific text types* focuses on text types that have unique vocabulary (for example, text messages and Twitter) and text types that should be read in a specific way (for example, step-by-step instructions or labels on medicine bottles).

- **Appendix 4:** *Understanding punctuation* explains some forms of English punctuation that you will see when you read.

- **Appendix 5:** *Understanding short forms in English* gives you some help with symbols that can be used in text messages, notes and on Twitter.
- **Appendix 6:** *Signposting language* shows the language that helps you to find your way around a text, for example, when an important point is being made.
- **Appendix 7:** *Using a dictionary* shows you how to use the information provided in the mini-dictionary entries.
- A mini-dictionary gives definitions and example sentences for some of the more difficult words in the units. Definitions are taken from Collins COBUILD dictionaries.
- A comprehensive answer key.

Using *Reading*

There are two ways to use this book:

1 Work through from units 1 to 20.
2 Choose from the Contents page (as trainer or learner) the units that are most useful or interesting to you.

Keep a vocabulary notebook and, after completing each unit, add any new words from the text to your book. You can use the mini-dictionary at the back to help you.

Language level

Reading has been written to help learners at A2 level and above (Pre-intermediate).

Other titles

Also available in the *Collins English for Life* series at A2 level: *Speaking, Listening* and *Writing*.

Available in the *Collins English for Life* series at B1 level: *Reading, Speaking, Listening* and *Writing*.

1 MEETING AND GREETING

Getting started

1 What do you use the Internet for?

2 Who do you chat to on the Internet?

3 What do you chat about?

A Meeting people online

1 You want to meet other people who are learning so you go to EnglishClub.com. Read the webpage *very quickly* and choose the best ending for the sentence.

On this webpage, people give their names and talk about ...

a what they like to do in their free time.

b where they come from and why they want to improve their English.

c the schools and colleges where they are learning English.

⌂ Home	Learn English	Teach English	My English Club

Get to know other students!

Mariana
Hello! My name's Mariana and I'm from Brazil. I love English and want to meet other people who love speaking English too! Send me a message if you want to chat.

Hannah
Hi, I'm Hannah and I come from France. I have English exams soon and I want to practise my English and make some new friends.

Pedro
Hello everyone! I'm Pedro, I'm Spanish and I live in Madrid. My girlfriend is English and I want to improve my language before I meet her family!

Li
Hey! My name is Li and I'm Chinese. I am going to live in America next year and I want to improve my English before I go! This is a great forum and I hope to make some new friends.

2 Answer the questions.

1 Who is going to take English exams soon? ....

2 Who has an English girlfriend? ....

3 Who is moving to America next year? ....

4 Who wants to meet other people who also love English? ....

3 Unjumble the phrases.

1 name's Hello! from My Brazil Mariana I'm and

2 Chinese My is Hey! Li and name I'm

3 Pedro, I'm I'm Hello Madrid live Spanish and everyone! I in

4 come Hi, Hannah I'm I France and from

B Getting to know somebody online

1 Read the conversation in the chat box. Are the sentences below true or false? Correct any that are false.

1 Ava comes from Germany, but lives in Brazil at the moment.
False. Ava is from Germany but lives in England at the moment.

2 Mariana likes living in Sao Paolo.

....

....

3 Ava plans to visit Sao Paolo next year for the carnival.

....

....

4 Mariana doesn't like the carnival.

....

....

5 Mariana is 27 years old.

....

....

6 Ava is busy tomorrow so won't be able to chat.

....

....

> **Ava:** Hi Mariana. I saw your post on EnglishClub. My name is Ava and I love talking in English too!
>
> **Mariana:** Hi Ava! Nice to meet you.
>
> **Ava:** Pleased to meet you too! How are you?
>
> **Mariana:** I'm fine, thanks ☺ Where are you from?
>
> **Ava:** I come from Germany, but I'm living in England atm. Where do you live in Brazil btw?
>
> **Mariana:** I live in Sao Paulo. It's a great city with lots of interesting people.
>
> **Ava:** Hey, I came to Sao Paulo last year for the carnival.
>
> **Mariana:** Ah, carnival is my favourite time of year! Did you like it?
>
> **Ava:** Yes it was amazing! How old are you, Mariana?
>
> **Mariana:** I'm 23. And you?
>
> **Ava:** 27. It's my first time on EnglishClub forum so thx for talking to me ☺
>
> **Mariana:** Well, it's been fun. Let's do it again soon. Got to go now. Maybe chat tomorrow same time?
>
> **Ava:** Yes pls! I'll be here.
>
> **Mariana:** cu

Language note: chat abbreviations

We often use abbreviations when we chat online. For example:

- atm = at the moment
- btw = by the way
- cu = see you
- pls = please
- thx = thanks

C Finding new friends online

1 You have just arrived in London and you don't know anyone. You read CitySocialising.com to find new friends. Read the webpage *very quickly*. What information does it give about each person? Write a ✓ or a ✗.

1 Name .... 4 Job ....

2 Age .... 5 Languages they speak ....

3 Nationality .... 6 Things they like to do in their free time ....

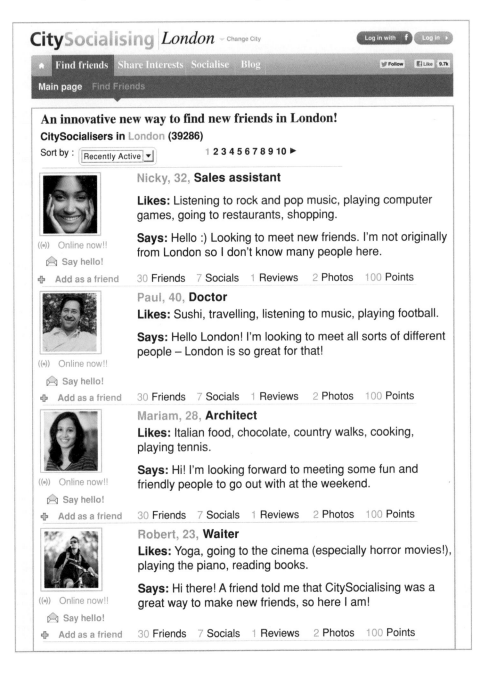

2 Answer the questions.

1 Who likes watching frightening films?   Robert

2 What does Nicky do? ....

3 How old is Mariam? ....

4 What sort of people does Paul want to meet? ....

5 Who likes eating chocolate? ....

6 Whose friend told them about CitySocialising? ....

Reading tip: keeping a vocabulary notebook

Reading is a great way of improving your vocabulary. When you have finished reading a text, go back over it and write down any useful new words in your vocabulary notebook. Try to learn a few new words every day. Test yourself by reading texts that you have read before to see if you can remember all the words.

3 Read what these people say. Who do you think they would most like to meet?

1 'I love playing tennis!' ....

2 'I want to find a yoga class' ....

3 'My favourite thing to do in my free time is shopping!' ....

4 'I love football! My favourite team is Manchester United.' ....

4 Who would you most like to meet? Complete the sentence.

I would most like to meet .... because ....

....

5 You decide to join CitySocialising.com. Complete your profile.

Name: .... Age: .... Job: ....

Likes: ....

Says: ....

My review

I can read introductions in Internet chatrooms.   ❏

I can understand personal information in online profiles.   ❏

I can get to know somebody by chatting online.   ❏

2 STAYING IN TOUCH

Getting started

1 How do you stay in touch with your friends?
2 What's your favourite social networking site and how often do you use it?
3 Do you prefer to email, text or phone your friends?

A Using social networking sites

1 Look at Friendsmeet on page 13, a new social networking site. Before you read, match the words to the meanings.

1	my status	a	where you can share things with your friends.
2	my profile	b	where you can read your messages.
3	my messages	c	where you can say something about your friend's status.
4	comment	d	where you can write about what you are doing or feeling.
5	share	e	where you can see personal information.

Reading tip: reading for particular information

When you are reading to find a particular piece of information, pass your eyes over the text quickly, stopping when you get to the important parts. For example, if you're looking for a name, stop when you see a capital letter.

---

2 You want to find out about three things from your friends. Read the questions then read Friendsmeet *very quickly* for the answers. Complete the table.

1 Has Mary had her baby yet?   2 Did Yiannis finish the marathon?   3 Is Max having a good birthday?

	Have they posted on Friendsmeet?	If Yes, what do they say?
Mary		
Yiannis		
Max		

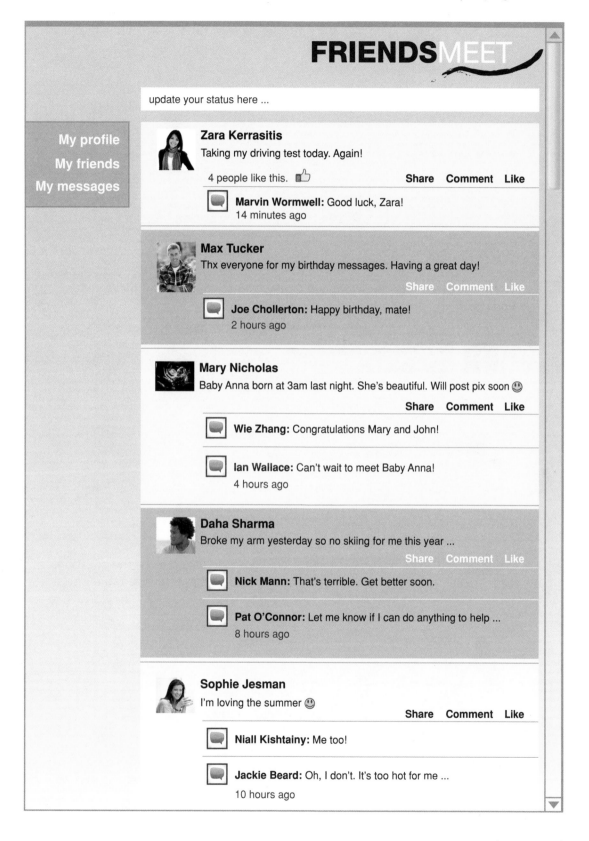

FRIENDSMEET

update your status here ...

Zara Kerrasitis
Taking my driving test today. Again!

4 people like this. 👍   Share   Comment   Like

💬 **Marvin Wormwell:** Good luck, Zara!
14 minutes ago

Max Tucker
Thx everyone for my birthday messages. Having a great day!

Share   Comment   Like

💬 **Joe Chollerton:** Happy birthday, mate!
2 hours ago

Mary Nicholas
Baby Anna born at 3am last night. She's beautiful. Will post pix soon 😊

Share   Comment   Like

💬 **Wie Zhang:** Congratulations Mary and John!

💬 **Ian Wallace:** Can't wait to meet Baby Anna!
4 hours ago

Daha Sharma
Broke my arm yesterday so no skiing for me this year ...

Share   Comment   Like

💬 **Nick Mann:** That's terrible. Get better soon.

💬 **Pat O'Connor:** Let me know if I can do anything to help ...
8 hours ago

Sophie Jesman
I'm loving the summer 😊

Share   Comment   Like

💬 **Niall Kishtainy:** Me too!

💬 **Jackie Beard:** Oh, I don't. It's too hot for me ...
10 hours ago

My profile
My friends
My messages

3 Read the webpage again. Are the sentences true or false? Correct any that are false.

1 Zara is taking her driving test for the first time today.
False. Zara is taking her driving test again today.

2 It is Max Tucker's birthday today.

....

3 Mary had a baby son last night.

....

4 Sophie Jesman broke her arm yesterday.

....

5 Jackie Beard doesn't like the summer.

....

4 Use expressions from the webpage on page 13 to comment on these status updates.

1

Mary Nicholas
I've got a new job!

Share   Comment   Like

Congratulations! ....

2

Daha Sharma
English exam today ...

Share   Comment   Like

....

3

Max Tucker
Someone has stolen my car!

Share   Comment   Like

....

4

Zara Kerrasitis
I love chocolate cake ☺

Share   Comment   Like

....

5

Sophie Jesman
27 today!

Share   Comment   Like

....

B Reading an email from a friend

1 You have an email from your friend Yiannis. Read it *very quickly* then look at the subject box. Underline what you think the main message will be.

Yiannis *finished / didn't* finish the marathon.

From	Yiannis K
Subject:	Good news!

Hi Kim,

Guess what ... I did it!!! I finished the marathon! My time was 3 hours 48 minutes so I'm very happy. And very tired ... Ben also finished – his time was 4 hours 32 minutes.

How are you? How are your English studies going?

Our house is VERY full at the moment because my sister and her husband are visiting. And they've brought their new dog with them! His name is Yiannis too! My sister thought it was funny to name him after me ...

See you soon,

Yiannis

2 Now read the email again and answer the questions.

1 How long did it take Yiannis to run the marathon?
   3 hours and 48 minutes

2 How long did it take Ben to run the marathon?
   ....

3 How is Yiannis feeling now?
   ....

4 Who is staying with Yiannis at the moment?
   ....

5 What is the name of his sister's new dog?
   ....

3 Reply to Yiannis's email. Remember to congratulate him and answer his questions.

My review

I can navigate the pages of a social networking site.	❑
I can read a social networking site quickly to find information about particular friends.	❑
I can use the right expressions when making comments on social networking sites.	❑
I can read an email quickly to understand its main message.	❑

3 MAKING PLANS

Getting started

1 What do you think this person is doing?

2 How do you usually make plans – by email, phone, text, or just by talking?

3 Where do you record your plans?

A Reading texts to plan a social activity

1 You are going to read some text messages. Before you read, match the text abbreviations with the words.

1	r	a	you are / you're / your
2	cu	b	tomorrow
3	ur	c	see you
4	4wd	d	today
5	2day	e	forward
6	2mro	f	are

Language note: text-speak smileys

We often use these smileys to show how we are feeling in our text messages:

:) OR  = I'm happy   :(OR ☹ = I'm sad

;) or ☺ = I'm joking   :-@ or ☹ = I'm angry

:-? or ☹ = I'm confused

Reading tip: reading numerals in text messages

Numerals can have more than one meaning in text messages, for example '2' can mean 'two', 'to' or 'too'. '4' can mean 'four' or 'for'. They can also form parts of words, for example '4wd' means 'forward' and 'l8' means 'late'.

Ru going 2 the party today? I want 2 go 2!

OK! I will 4wd the invitation 2 u l8r!

2   Read the text messages between Leila and Sophia. Answer the questions.

> Hi Sophia, r u free 2day
> 4 coffee and chat? ☺ L x

> Sorry Leila, busy 2day. ☹
> What abt 2mro?

> Morning is ok. Where do u
> want 2 meet?

> Come to my hse? 2 tired
> 2 go out! ☺
> Also, got to be home
> 4 a delivery in the morning.

> No probs, what time
> gd 4 u?

> 10.30? Can I c ur holiday pix?
> Planning 2 go 2 Greece and
> want 2 c what it's like! S x

> Sure! Look 4wd 2 seeing
> u! L x

1   Why does Leila text Sophia?

To suggest meeting today for a coffee and a chat.

2   When do they plan to meet?

....

3   Where do they plan to meet?

....

4   Why must Sophia be at home tomorrow morning?

....

5   What does Sophia ask to see and why?

....

3   Read the text messages. What do they say?

1   r u free 2day 4 coffee? = Are *you* free today *for* a coffee?

2   Sorry, busy 2day. = Sorry, I .... busy ....

3   What abt 2mro? = What ....?

4   What time gd 4 u? = What time is .... for ....?

5   Can I c ur holiday pix? = Can I .... holiday ....?

6   Look 4wd 2 seeing u! = I'll look .... to seeing ....!

B Reading a group email

1 Read the group email *very quickly* then choose the best subject for the group email. Start with the earliest email (at the bottom).

- your birthday party!
- Saturday night...
- Holiday plans!

To   Sophia, Mei
Subject:

Yes, I can do the first week of September. We're going to have such a good time!

xx

From: Mei
To: Sophia; Erika
Sent: 3 June 14:12
Subject:

Oh, Greece is a great idea! I'm going to visit friends in Denmark in July, but the first week of September is good for me. Erika – can you do September? Let's get together next week to plan it.

Soooooo excited!

Love

Mei x

From: Sophia
To: Erika; Mei
Sent: 3 June 11:18
Subject:

I am definitely still interested in going away together! How about Greece? I was looking at my friend's photos today and it looks great. I can't do August because I'm going to Rome, but I might be free at the start of September.

Mei, what are your plans?

S x

From: Erika
To: Sophia; Mei
Sent: 3 June 11:13
Subject:

Hi girls!

Right, we need to start planning our summer or all the holidays will be booked up ... are you both still up for going away together somewhere? July is no good for me because I'm working but I can do August? How about you two?

Is August good for you? And where are we going to go? We talked about somewhere hot and sunny, didn't we? But where?!

Erika xx

---

2 Read the emails again. Are the sentences true or false? Correct any that are false.

1 Erika, Sophia and Mei are going to go to Greece for their holidays this year.
True.

2 Erika is not free to go in August.

....

3 Mei suggests that they go to Greece.

....

4 Sophia is not free to go on holiday in August because she's going to Rome.

....

5 Mei thinks it's a bad idea to go to Greece.

....

Language note: informal emails

The language of informal emails is often closer to spoken English than written English, for example:

Sooooooo excited = I'm so excited
How about Greece? = What do you think about Greece?
How about you two? = What do you two think?

---

3 Complete the table with phrases from the emails for making plans.

1 To ask if somebody is free

    a *is August good for you?*   **b** ....

2 To say that you are free

    a ....   **b** ....

3 To say that you aren't free

    a ....   **b** *I can't do August.*

4 You can use the present continuous OR 'going to' to talk about future plans. Complete the sentences showing both ways of writing these forms.

1 I'm *having / going to have* (have) dinner with my brother tonight.

2 I .... (visit) Rome next week.

3 We .... (stay) with friends in France over Christmas.

4 He .... (go) to Greece this September.

5 My friends .... (meet) me in town.

My review

I can understand text abbreviations.	❑
I can follow a group conversation by email.	❑
I can understand useful phrases to make plans.	❑

4 UNDERSTANDING OPINIONS

Getting started

1 How do you think this person feels?
2 Do you like to tell your friends your opinions or do you prefer to talk about them online to people you don't know?
3 Where can you give your opinion online?

A Using Twitter

1 Twitter is a website where users can read and post short messages. Complete the sentences using the words in the box.

Tweet	Tweets	Retweet	follow	followers

1 The short 140-character messages are called ....

2 If you usually read somebody's Tweets, you .... them.

3 At the moment, Lady Gaga has the most .... – over 30 million people.

4 If a person has written a .... , it means they have posted a message.

5 When you .... something, you post a message that was written earlier by another user.

Reading tip: using Twitter to practise reading

Follow some English-speaking celebrities who you admire to make your timeline more interesting as well as practising reading in English. For example:

- @BarackObama
- @WayneRooney
- @ladygaga
- @TheBritishMonarchy

2 Read the Twitter page *very quickly*. What is being talked about? Write a ✓ or a ✗.

1 Leah Potts's new film ....
2 Martin James's new book ....
3 The President of the USA ....
4 Last night's football match between Manchester Utd and Juventus ....
5 The Beatbops on Talent Showcase ....
6 A new book ....

🏠 Home   @Connect   #Discover   👤 Me   Search 🔍   ⚙ ▾   ✉

Stephen Carter
View my profile page

143	**118**	**93**
TWEETS	FOLLOWING	FOLLOWERS

Compose new Tweet...

Who to follow • Refresh • View all

ChrisHowOman   x
Followed by
Nicole Peters

Cassie Phillips   x
Followed by
JamesKiteBroms

SweensUrbanDes   x
Followed by
Ruth Hammond

Worldwide Trends • Change
#RunForLife
#10peopleIwanttomeet
#LeahPotts
#FavoriteTVshow
RIP Francis Harrod
La Dolce Vita
Father's day
Welcome to Japan Justin
Shopping or sleeping?
Lewis Peel

🐦

© 2012 Twitter About Help Terms Privacy
Blog Status Apps Resources Jobs
Advertisers Businesses Media Developers

Tweets

Films for you @FilmsForYou   2m
New film from #LeahPotts, When Night Comes,
is now showing at cinemas. To find out more,
go to www.filmsforyou.com

WRC News @WRCNewsCorp   3m
Breaking news: President of the United States
in official visit to Argentina. For full story,
go to: www.wrcnews.com

Jason Hart @jason-hart22   1h
Leah Potts is trending worldwide! Yay!! I love her
and I adore her movies. When Night Comes –
she's a great actress! #LeahPotts

Spyros Nicolaou @spyrosnicolaou   2h
@Beatbopno1fan I hate the Beatbops!
I thought they were awful on Talent Showcase!
Liana De La Paz was good, though! Vote for
#Liana instead!

Beatbopno1fan @Beatbopno1fan   2h
I really like The Beatbops!!! They were amazing
on Talent Showcase. Vote to keep them in the
show on 05339 3994 444!!!!

HarperCollins @HarperCollins   3h
Latest edition of Collins Easy Learning English
Vocabulary now available. To find out more
go to: www.collinselt.com

Emilie Carreau @EmilieCarreau   3h
Collins Easy Learning English Vocabulary is very
good and really helped me to improve my English!
↻ Retweeted by Collins Language

Kurt Freyer @freyerkurt   3h
Someone explain to me why Leah Potts is
trending??????!!!! I can't stand her! She's a bad
actress and her new film is terrible!! #LeahPotts

Kim Kid DJ @KimKidDJ   3h
Hey! I'm on Radio Soundwaves tomorrow between
10.00 and 12.00. Tweet me songs you want me to
play!

MusicLoversUnite @MusicLoversUnite   3h
We really enjoyed Steve The Hat's new single,
Show Me. Listen to it here www.stevethehat.com
and let us know what you think.
↻ Retweeted by Kim Kid DJ

3 For each Tweet, decide if it contains an opinion (one person's view about something) and/or a fact (something that is definitely true).

		opinion	fact
1	Films for you	....	✓
2	WRC News	....	....
3	Jason Hart	....	....
4	Spyros Nicolaou	....	....
5	Beatbopno1fan	....	....
6	Collins Language	....	....
7	Emilie Carreau	....	....
8	Kurt Freyer	....	....
9	Kim Kid DJ	....	....
10	MusicLoversUnite	....	....

4 Complete the lists with positive or negative phrases from the Tweets.

Positive phrases (things I like)	Negative phrases (things I don't like)
yay!! I love her ...	I hate the ...
....	....
....	....
....	....
....	....
....	....
....	....

B   Reading opinions in blogs

1 A blog is a website where people (known as bloggers) write their opinions about something. Before you read this blog by an English teacher, match the words to their meanings.

1	cool	a	a story that is not real
2	fiction	b	make better
3	improve	c	not natural
4	artificial	d	something inside another thing
5	contain	e	good, great

2 Read the blog *very quickly* then choose the best title.

1   Why grammar is better than fiction

2   Boring grammar or interesting fiction – you choose!

3   Don't read books!

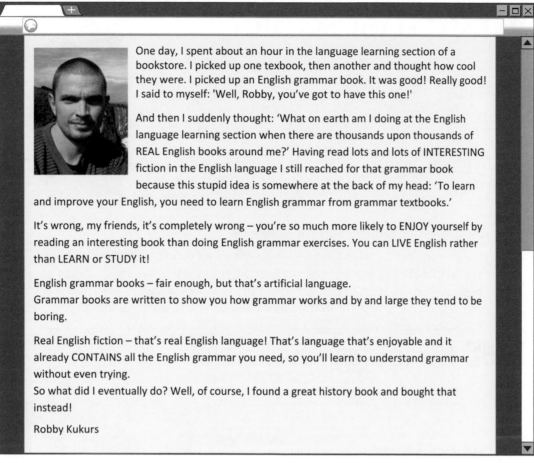

One day, I spent about an hour in the language learning section of a bookstore. I picked up one texbook, then another and thought how cool they were. I picked up an English grammar book. It was good! Really good! I said to myself: 'Well, Robby, you've got to have this one!'

And then I suddenly thought: 'What on earth am I doing at the English language learning section when there are thousands upon thousands of REAL English books around me?' Having read lots and lots of INTERESTING fiction in the English language I still reached for that grammar book because this stupid idea is somewhere at the back of my head: 'To learn and improve your English, you need to learn English grammar from grammar textbooks.'

It's wrong, my friends, it's completely wrong – you're so much more likely to ENJOY yourself by reading an interesting book than doing English grammar exercises. You can LIVE English rather than LEARN or STUDY it!

English grammar books – fair enough, but that's artificial language.
Grammar books are written to show you how grammar works and by and large they tend to be boring.

Real English fiction – that's real English language! That's language that's enjoyable and it already CONTAINS all the English grammar you need, so you'll learn to understand grammar without even trying.
So what did I eventually do? Well, of course, I found a great history book and bought that instead!

Robby Kukurs

Article adapted from authentic blog post by Robby Kukurs (http://englishharmony.com)

3 **Read these visitor comments on Robby's blog. Which do you think Robby agrees with? Write a ✓ or a ✗.**

1 I love reading fiction in English – it's great for improving your vocabulary and fluency! ....

2 I really like grammar and I think it's the best way to learn any language! ....

3 I do read a lot of books in English, but I think studying grammar is the best way to improve your language. ....

4 I always tell my students, go to an English-speaking country, live the language – it's much more interesting than having your head stuck in a grammar book! ....

5 I can't stand grammar books – I prefer good fiction! ....

My review

I can read a Twitter page quickly to see what is being talked about. ❑

I can tell the difference between a fact and an opinion. ❑

I can read a blog quickly to find out what it's about. ❑

5 REGISTERING AT A LANGUAGE SCHOOL

Getting started

1 Have you ever studied at a language school abroad?
2 How would you find out about language schools abroad?
3 What kind of texts might you read when you arrive at a language school?

A   Reading a language school website

1 You are looking for a language school online and you find the English Made Easy School (EME). You want to study an intensive general English course at Pre-intermediate level in London. Read the webpage *very quickly*. Does this school offer the course you want in the place you want? Is it worth reading on?

EME Language Schools
English Made Easy

`Search` 🔍 💬

About us   **Our courses**   Prices   Accommodation   Book online

• Accredited by the Language Learning Council

• Excellent qualified teachers

• Study at our schools in **London**, **Edinburgh** or **Dublin**

• Full social programme available

At **EME Language Schools**, we offer a wide variety of different courses. You are sure to find one that suits you!

EXAM ENGLISH
• Cambridge Exam Preparation Courses: FCE / CAE / CPE
• TOEIC Exam Preparation Course
• IELTS Exam Preparation Course

GENERAL ENGLISH
• Available at six levels: Beginner (sometimes available – contact us to check), Elementary, Pre-intermediate, Intermediate, Upper-intermediate, Advanced
• Standard (20 hrs/week); intensive (28 hrs/week); 1:1 courses available

ESP (English for specific purposes)
• Business English
• English for Tourism

FAQs   Terms & Conditions   Contact us

---

2   You tell your friends about EME. Read the website again and answer their questions.

1	Do they do exam preparation courses for IELTS?	Yes / No
2	Do they run Advanced courses?	Yes / No
3	Do they teach English for Law?	Yes / No
4	Do they have a school in Manchester?	Yes / No
5	Can you book online?	Yes / No
6	Do they organise social activities?	Yes / No

B   Understanding an online registration form

1   You decide to book online at EME. Before you read the registration form, match the words to the meanings.

1	surname	**a**	the day, month and year that you were born
2	nationality	**b**	family name
3	date of birth	**c**	place to stay
4	accommodation	**d**	the country that you are from

Language note: common abbreviations

Abbreviations are often used in registration forms.

Sex: M   F = Sex: Male   Female   **DOB** = Date of birth

         St = Street   **n/a** = not applicable (not relevant)

---

2   Read your friend's registration form then answer the questions on the next page.

EME SCHOOLS REGISTRATION FORM

First name: Ludmila   Surname: Petrova

Sex: M (F)   Nationality: Russian

Email: lpetrova@mailshot.com   DOB: 27/06/1993

Home telephone number: +7903 790 5588   Work telephone number: n/a

Address: Nevsky St 4/24, Moscow, 113105, Russia

Which EME School would you like to attend: London ⦿   Edinburgh ○   Dublin ○

How long have you studied English for: 4   years   3   months

First language: Russian

Select your English level: Beginner ○   Pre-intermediate ○   Intermediate ○   Upper-intermediate ⦿   Advanced ○

Do you require EME Schools to organize accommodation with a host family?   Yes ⦿   No ○

1 Where is Ludmila from?

Russia

2 When was she born?

....

3 Where is she going to stay while in London?

....

4 What is Ludmila's level of English?

....

5 How long has she been studying English?

....

3 Complete the registration form with your own details.

EME SCHOOLS REGISTRATION FORM

First name: [   ]   Surname: [   ]

Sex: [M   F]   Nationality: [   ]

Email: [   ]   DOB: [   ]

Home telephone number: [   ]   Work telephone number: [   ]

Address: [   ]

Which EME School would you like to attend: London ○   Edinburgh ○   Dublin ○

How long have you studied English for: [ ] years ⬍ [ ] months ⬍

First language: [   ]

Select your English level: Beginner ○ Pre-intermediate ○ Intermediate ○ Upper-intermediate ○ Advanced ○

Do you require EME Schools to organize accommodation with a host family? Yes ○   No ○

C   Reading a noticeboard

1 You arrive at the language school and see the noticeboard. What are the notices about? Write a ✓ or a ✗.

1 Accommodation   ....

2 Day trips   ....

3 Weekend trips to Europe   ....

4 Extra speaking lessons   ....

5 The school website information ....

6 Meeting other students   ....

GREAT DAYS OUT
EXPLORE AMAZING PLACES
less than three hours from London...

Visit Blenheim Palace or Windsor Castle or go to the old universities of Oxford or Cambridge.

Travel by luxury air-conditioned coach with pick-ups from the language school.

For details of dates and prices, go to www.greatdaysout.co.uk or call 021 293 1002

COFFEE MORNING

New to EME?

See you there!

Come and make new friends and practise your English!

We meet on the first Saturday of each month, at 10 a.m. in the school café.

Extra help with your spoken English!

Call Margaret on 01090 292 294 to arrange private one-to-one lessons.

Only £15/hr.

All levels.

2 Read the notices again. Are the sentences true or false? Write a ✓ in the correct place.

		True	False
1	Great Days Out organize day trips to places within three hours of London.	✓	
2	Great Days Out organize trips by train.		
3	Margaret offers private lessons to students of all levels.		
4	Margaret's lessons cost £15 for 30 minutes.		
5	The coffee morning happens every Saturday at 10am.		
6	The coffee morning takes place in the school café.		

My review

I can read a website quickly to see if it's useful.	☐
I can understand information about language schools and courses.	☐
I can complete online registration forms.	☐
I can understand information on noticeboards.	☐

6 ARRIVING AT A HOTEL

Getting started

1 Have you stayed in a hotel before?

2 Where was the last hotel you stayed? What was it like?

3 What facilities did the hotel have?

A Reading about a hotel

1 You arrive at a hotel and see the leaflet below. Read the leaflet *very quickly*. Does it have these facilities? Write a ✓ or a ✗.

1 Room service   ....
2 A safe in your room   ....
3 Film rental   ....

4 Free Internet access ....
5 Jacuzzi   ....
6 Swimming pool   ....

Welcome to Hotel Imperial

We hope you enjoy your stay! Here is some information to help you to get the most out of your visit.

Room facilities
telephone
free wi-fi, safe, room service
minibar, cable TV with over 100 channels
air-conditioning and individual heating controls

Fitness centre
Opening hours 07.00–22.00 daily
fully-equipped gym
indoor swimming pool
sauna and steam room
massages available – contact reception

Breakfast Served in The Menard Restaurant
Monday to Friday, 06:30–09:30
Saturday and Sunday, 07:00–10:00

Other facilities: left-luggage room, conference facilities, wheelchair accessible
If you need any extra information, dial 0 to speak to reception at any time.

---

2 Complete the sentences using the words in the box.

facilities	access	fully equipped	available	reception

1 All visitors have .... to the gym – they can go there.

2 The gym is .... – it has a lot of exercise machines.

3 The hotel has many ...., e.g. swimming pool, gym, restaurant and conference centre.

4 Wi-fi is .... – you can use it free of charge.

5 If you have any questions, ask at .... – they will help you.

3 Read the leaflet again. Choose the correct answer.

1 You *can / can't* get a drink from the minibar in your room.

2 You *can / can't* eat breakfast on Sunday at 09:45.

3 You *can / can't* have lunch on Thursday at 14:00.

4 There *is / isn't* a swimming pool.

5 There *is / isn't* a bar.

6 You *can / can't* leave your bags in the left-luggage room.

B Understanding notices

There is a notice on your hotel room door. Before you read it, match the words to the meanings.

1 discover   **a** go

2 suspect   **b** find

3 operate   **c** your things

4 proceed   **d** meeting place

5 assembly point   **e** think something is true

6 personal belongings   **f** work, make something work

2 Read the notice (on the next page) *very quickly*, then choose the correct answers.

1 What does the notice tell you?

    a What time breakfast is served.

    b What to do if there is a fire.

    c How to operate the TV in your room.

2 How important is the notice?

    a Very important. I'll read it carefully now.

    b Quite important. I'll look at it later.

    c Not important. I'm not going to read it carefully.

Fire action

IF YOU DISCOVER OR SUSPECT A FIRE

Fire door keep shut — Leave the room shutting the door behind you.

Operate the fire alarm using the nearest available call point.

ON HEARING THE ALARM
Leave the building IMMEDIATELY

Go to the assembly point at:
Oxford Street

Do not stop to collect personal belongings.
Do not re-enter the building.

3 Read the notice again and answer your friend's questions.

1 What do I do if there's a fire in my room?
Leave the room, shut the door behind you, and press the nearest fire alarm button.

2 What do I do if I hear the fire alarm?
....

3 Where exactly do I need to go?
....

4 Shall I take my bags with me?
....

5 Can I go back for my bags?
....

C Reading the weather forecast

1 You are staying in London until Friday. Read the weather forecast *very quickly*.
Which is the best day to go on a river cruise?

....

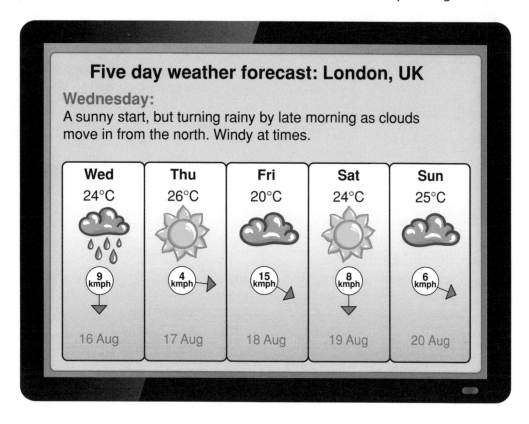

Five day weather forecast: London, UK

Wednesday:
A sunny start, but turning rainy by late morning as clouds move in from the north. Windy at times.

Wed	Thu	Fri	Sat	Sun
24°C	26°C	20°C	24°C	25°C
9 kmph	4 kmph	15 kmph	8 kmph	6 kmph
16 Aug	17 Aug	18 Aug	19 Aug	20 Aug

2 Read the weather forecast again. Are the sentences true or false? Write a ✓ in the correct place.

	True ✓	False
1 The windiest day will be Friday.	✓	....
2 The coldest day will be Thursday.	....	....
3 It will be cloudy on Friday and Sunday.	....	....
4 It will only be rainy on Wednesday.	....	....
5 It will be sunny on three days.	....	....

My review

I can read information about a hotel quickly to see what facilities are available. ☐

I can read a fire action notice carefully to know what to do if there is a fire. ☐

I can read a weather forecast to help plan my week. ☐

7 SIGHTSEEING

Getting started

1 Have you ever been to New York?
2 When you visit a new place, where do you like to go?
3 How do you find out about interesting places to visit?

A Planning your trip

1 You are planning a trip to New York and look online to find interesting places to visit. Before you read, complete the sentences using the letters in the box.

b	w	m	d	u

1 We went on a to….r of New York – the guide showed us the most famous places in the city.
2 We saw a musical perfor….ance in the park – the band played some great music.
3 We visited the new exhi….it – there were so many interesting things to look at.
4 We loved the vie…s from The Rockefeller Center – we could see for miles.
5 The Chrysler Building is a New York lan….mark – one of the best-known places in the city.

Language note: American English and British English

Did you know that American English is sometimes different from British English?

- Some words are spelt differently, for example 'center' instead of 'centre'.
- Some words are completely different, for example 'exhibit' instead of 'exhibition'.

---

2 Read the introduction to the website on page 33 *very quickly*. Choose the best title for it.

> Top five places for kids in NYC

> Top five cheap places to visit in NYC

> Top five free places to visit in NYC

3 Read the rest of the webpage and answer the questions.

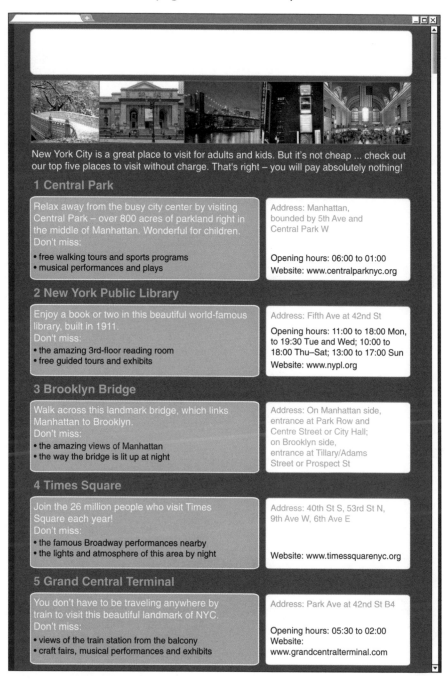

New York City is a great place to visit for adults and kids. But it's not cheap ... check out our top five places to visit without charge. That's right – you will pay absolutely nothing!

1 Central Park

Relax away from the busy city center by visiting Central Park – over 800 acres of parkland right in the middle of Manhattan. Wonderful for children.
Don't miss:
• free walking tours and sports programs
• musical performances and plays

Address: Manhattan, bounded by 5th Ave and Central Park W

Opening hours: 06:00 to 01:00
Website: www.centralparknyc.org

2 New York Public Library

Enjoy a book or two in this beautiful world-famous library, built in 1911.
Don't miss:
• the amazing 3rd-floor reading room
• free guided tours and exhibits

Address: Fifth Ave at 42nd St
Opening hours: 11:00 to 18:00 Mon, to 19:30 Tue and Wed; 10:00 to 18:00 Thu–Sat; 13:00 to 17:00 Sun
Website: www.nypl.org

3 Brooklyn Bridge

Walk across this landmark bridge, which links Manhattan to Brooklyn.
Don't miss:
• the amazing views of Manhattan
• the way the bridge is lit up at night

Address: On Manhattan side, entrance at Park Row and Centre Street or City Hall; on Brooklyn side, entrance at Tillary/Adams Street or Prospect St

4 Times Square

Join the 26 million people who visit Times Square each year!
Don't miss:
• the famous Broadway performances nearby
• the lights and atmosphere of this area by night

Address: 40th St S, 53rd St N, 9th Ave W, 6th Ave E

Website: www.timessquarenyc.org

5 Grand Central Terminal

You don't have to be traveling anywhere by train to visit this beautiful landmark of NYC.
Don't miss:
• views of the train station from the balcony
• craft fairs, musical performances and exhibits

Address: Park Ave at 42nd St B4

Opening hours: 05:30 to 02:00
Website: www.grandcentralterminal.com

1 How big is Central Park?
Over 800 acres

2 What time does Central Park open?

....

3 When was New York Public Library built?

....

4 Which two areas of New York does Brooklyn Bridge link?

....

5 How many people visit Times Square every year?

....

6 Where exactly is Grand Central Station?

....

4 Which places might these people like to visit?

1 I love books more than anything!

....

2 I really like big open spaces.

....

3 I love seeing shows and performances of any kind.

..../.../.....................................

4 I'm really interested in trains.

....

5 I like sightseeing at night. Cities really come to life after dark!

..../...

6 I enjoy looking at beautiful views.

..../...

5 Which place would you like to visit? Complete the sentence.

I'd like to visit .... because ....

....

Reading tip: using search engines

There are probably over 9 billion webpages on the internet, so it is important that you know how to find the best information.

- Write as many key words as you can in a search engine to make the results as useful as possible.

- When you click on a search result, pass your eyes over the webpage quickly looking for key words to see if the page is useful.

- If it is useful then take the time to read it carefully, but if it isn't then move onto the next page in the search result.

B   Visiting a museum

1 You are going to visit the Portman Museum. Before you read the webpage, match the words to the meanings.

1	admission	**a**	a card to show who you are and when you were born
2	adult	**b**	the money you pay to get in somewhere
3	senior	**c**	the money that is taken off a price
4	valid ID	**d**	a person who is over 60 years old
5	discount	**e**	a person who is over 18 years old

2 This webpage shows one page of the Portman Museum website. Read it *very quickly*. Does this page give the following information?

1 What there is to see at the museum. ....   **3** How to become a member. ....

2 What times the museum is open. ....   **4** How much it costs. ....

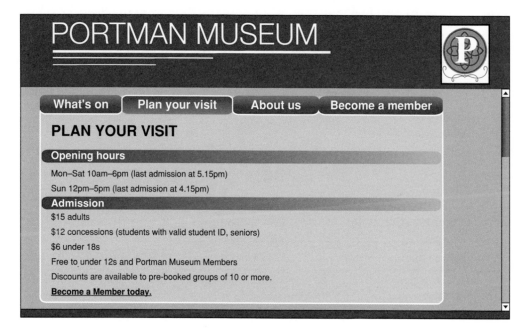

3 Underline the correct answer.

1 The museum opens at *10am / 12pm / 6pm* on Thursdays.

2 Last admission on Sundays is *4.15pm / 5pm / 5.15pm*.

3 Admission for one senior, one teenager (aged 13) and one child (aged 6) is *$18 / $21 / $27*.

4 Admission for two adult Portman Members is *free / $24 / $30*.

5 A group of *four / eight / twelve* people get a discount.

My review

I can read a tourist website or brochure to find an interesting place to visit.   ❑

I can understand information about opening times and admission prices.   ❑

8 GOING SHOPPING

Getting started

1 Do you like going shopping?
2 What's your favourite type of shop?
3 What are the people in the picture reading?
4 What do you read when you go shopping?

A Reading signs in shop windows

1 Where can you buy these things? Choose the shop from the box.

bakery	butcher	chemist	supermarket	gift shop	department store

1 medicines and toiletries
....

2 cakes and bread
....

3 meat
....

4 clothes, cosmetics and furniture
....

5 food and things for the house
....

6 presents and birthday cards
....

2 Complete the sentences using the words in the box.

sale	stock	price	reduction	allowed

1 All the things that a shop sells are the shop's ....
2 The .... is the amount of money that you have to pay for something.
3 If something is ...., then you can do it.
4 If there is a ...., then things in a shop cost less money than normal.
5 When something sells for less than normal, there is a .... in the price.

3 You go shopping and see these signs in shop windows. What do they mean? Read the signs and choose the best answer.

1   a   The shop is now closed – you must leave.

    b   We are selling everything cheaply because the shop
        will soon close and it will not re-open.

2 **a** We have lots of new things in the shop.

    b We have lots of new people in the shop.

3 **a** We are selling things in the shop for less than normal.

    b We are selling things in the shop for more than normal.

4 **a** You pay for one thing and you get two things.

    b You pay for one thing and you get three things.

5 **a** Dogs can come in here.

    b Dogs can't come in here.

6 **a** You can use wifi here without paying any money.

    b You can use wifi here if nobody else is using it at the same time.

Reading tip: read wherever you are!

Reading is not something that you can only do in the classroom. When you're in an English country, you can practise reading wherever you are – look out for signs and notices in windows as you walk around town. What signs do you see in shops, restaurants, cafés or hotels? Look up any new words and write them in your vocabulary notebook.

B Buying something in a shop

1 You buy a present in a gift shop. At the till, you see a notice. Before you read it, match the beginnings to the ends of the sentences.

1	A return	**a**	is when you swap something that you have bought for something else.
2	A refund	**b**	is when you take something back to a shop because you don't want to keep it.
3	An exchange	**c**	is money that is returned to you when you have paid more than the item costs.
4	Your change	**d**	is the piece of paper that you get when you buy something to show that you have paid for it.
5	A receipt	**e**	is when you take something back to a shop and they give you your money back.

2 While you are waiting to pay, another customer asks you some questions about the notice. Answer her questions.

PAYMENT METHODS
We accept the following methods of payment:
Cash and all major credit cards
(except for RCH credit cards)

RETURNS POLICY
If you are not completely satisfied with your item, simply return it to us unopened, together with your receipt, within 14 days of purchase for an exchange or full refund.

1 Can I pay by RCH credit card?
No, you can't.

2 If my daughter doesn't like it, can I bring it back and get my money back?
....

3 I won't be able to get back to the shop for three weeks. Will it be OK to bring it back then?
....

4 Do I need to keep the receipt?
....

5 Can I bring it back if it's been opened?
....

3 You buy two items. One costs £2.99 and the other is £10. You pay with a £20 note. Read your receipt and circle the mistake.

```
Gifts 4 u
Stoke Newington
N16 4RS
Tel: 0207 283 1992
Cashier: Drew Till: B
Vat no: 28399402
----------------------------------------
Bath Oil                         £3.99
Photograph frame                £10.00
TOTAL                           £13.99
CASH                            £20.00
Change                           £6.01
----------------------------------------
Date:16 March Time: 11:14
Thank you for shopping with us!
Please keep your receipt.
Visit www.gifts4u.co.uk
to sign up for our free newsletter.
```

4 Answer the questions.

1 What's the name of the shop?

....

2 What's the name of the cashier who sold you the things?

....

3 What was the date and time that you bought the presents?

..../...

4 What's the last date that you can return the items and get your money back?

....

5 What can you sign up for at the gift shop website?

....

My review

I can understand signs in shop windows.   ❑

I can read notices about returning items.   ❑

I can check that a receipt is correct.   ❑

9 EATING OUT

Getting started

1 What are these people doing?
2 What restaurants do you like going to?
3 How do you choose which restaurant to go to?
4 What do you read when you are in a restaurant?

A Deciding where to eat

1 You are in San Francisco. You look at some restaurant reviews online. Before you read, match the place to the type of food it serves.

1	Diner	a	East/South Asian
2	Curry house	b	American
3	Noodle bar	c	Italian
4	Pizzeria	d	Indian

2 Read the website *very quickly* then check your answers to Exercise A1.

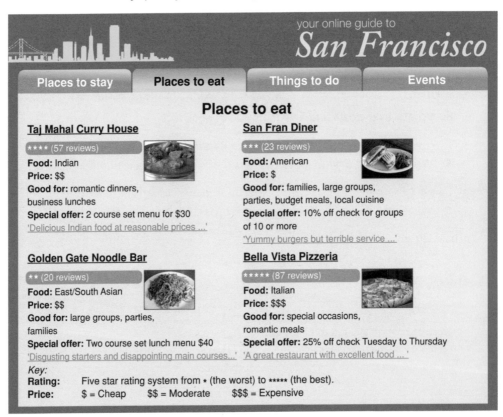

your online guide to
San Francisco

| Places to stay | **Places to eat** | Things to do | Events |

Places to eat

Taj Mahal Curry House

★★★★ (57 reviews)
Food: Indian
Price: $$
Good for: romantic dinners, business lunches
Special offer: 2 course set menu for $30
'Delicious Indian food at reasonable prices ...'

Golden Gate Noodle Bar

★★ (20 reviews)
Food: East/South Asian
Price: $$
Good for: large groups, parties, families
Special offer: Two course set lunch menu $40
'Disgusting starters and disappointing main courses...'

San Fran Diner

★★★ (23 reviews)
Food: American
Price: $
Good for: families, large groups, parties, budget meals, local cuisine
Special offer: 10% off check for groups of 10 or more
'Yummy burgers but terrible service ...'

Bella Vista Pizzeria

★★★★★ (87 reviews)
Food: Italian
Price: $$$
Good for: special occasions, romantic meals
Special offer: 25% off check Tuesday to Thursday
'A great restaurant with excellent food ... '

Key:
Rating: Five star rating system from ★ (the worst) to ★★★★★ (the best).
Price: $ = Cheap $$ = Moderate $$$ = Expensive

3 Read the reviews again and suggest a restaurant or restaurants to these people.

1 I want to go to the place with the highest star rating.
Bella Vista Pizzeria

2 We don't have much money and are travelling on a very small budget.

....

3 I'm eating out with my kids.

..../...

4 I'm planning a romantic meal with my wife.

..../...

5 I love pizza – Italian food is my favourite!

....

6 I always like to taste the local food of the place I'm staying. Here in San Francisco, that means I'm looking for a great burger!

....

4 Write the adjectives under the correct heading.

delicious	yummy	terrible	disgusting	disappointing	excellent

Good			
Bad			

B Reading the menu

1 Complete the food labels.

1	2	3	4
b...r..........	...e...t......e	f..........s	t...m......o

5	6	7	8
...t......k	i...e-...r......m	ch......s...	g...r...ic

2 Read the menu *very quickly*. Which restaurant does it belong to? Complete the menu with the restaurant's name.

THE ....

MENU

Appetizers

Shrimp cocktail — $7.95
Boiled shrimps served with a delicious homemade cocktail sauce

Chicken wings — $6.95
Deep-fried chicken wings served with a sweet & sour sauce

Potato skins — $5.95
Deep-fried potato skins served with a spicy mayonnaise dip

Mains

San Fran House Special: Steak sandwich — $9.95
Grilled 9oz steak served with mayonnaise, lettuce, onions & fries

Chef's Original Burger — $7.95
The classic burger served in a bun with tomatoes & onions
with cheese — $8.95

Tuna salad — $8.95
Freshly made salad with tuna, lettuce, cucumber, olives & egg

San Jose omelette — $8.95
A classic American omelette with mushrooms, bell peppers & cheese

Sides

Basket of fries — $2.95
Bowl of onion rings — $3.95
Garlic bread — $2.95

Desserts

3-scoop ice cream sundae — $3.95
Lemon meringue pie — $4.95
Pineapple cheesecake — $5.95

Soft drinks

Cola and lemonade (free refills!) — $1.95
Fresh orange juice — Reg $2.75 Lge: $3.75
Coffee (free refills!) — $1.95

Service not included! (For groups of 10 or more, a discretionary 15% tip will be added to your check).

3 Are the sentences true or false? Correct any that are false.

1 Chicken wings are served with a spicy mayonnaise dip.
False. They are served with a sweet and sour sauce.

2 A Chef's Original Burger with cheese costs $9.95

....

3   You can also order fries, garlic bread or salad.

....

4   You can have free refills of cola, lemonade and coffee.

....

5   Fresh orange juice comes in three sizes: small, regular or large.

....

6   Service is not included for a group of six people.

....

Language note: American English and British English

Did you notice the American words used in the menu?

American	British
appetizers	starters
shrimp	prawn
fries	chips
check	bill

---

4   **Your friends are late and ask you to order for them. Complete the sentences.**

1   Jane is vegetarian. I'll order her the *potato skins* for appetizer and the ....
for main.

2   Lee loves fish. I'll order him the .... for appetizer and the .... for
main.

3   Kim likes meat, especially steak so I'll order her the .... for appetizer and the
.... for main.

4   And as for me, well let's see, I'll have the .... for appetizer and the
.... for main.

5   **Match the beginnings to the ends of the sentences.**

1   Boiled food is cooked ...   **a**   in oil in a frying pan.

2   Fried food is cooked ...   **b**   in lots of water in a saucepan.

3   Baked food is cooked ...   **c**   under a grill or on a barbecue.

4   Grilled food is cooked ...   **d**   in an oven.

My review

I can read reviews to find a good restaurant.	❑
I can choose what to eat from a menu.	❑
I can understand words for different foods and different ways of cooking.	❑

10 GOING TO THE CINEMA

Getting started

1 How often do you go to the cinema?
2 What sort of films do you like to watch?
3 How do you choose what film to watch?

A Choosing a film

 You want to go to the cinema, so you read some film reviews to decide which film to see. Read the reviews *very quickly* then match the films to the descriptions.

1 A Royal Affair ...

2 Prometheus ...

a is a science fiction film set in the future.

b is a historical drama set in the past.

What's on
by Kate Muir

A Royal Affair
Director: Nikolaj Arcel
(128 min)
★★★★☆
An excellent Danish drama about passion and politics, this is the true story of the 18th century king of Denmark Christian VII whose doctor (played by the superb actor Mads Mikkelsen) falls in love with the Queen. A long, slow pleasure.

Prometheus
Director: Ridley Scott
(125 min)
★★★★☆
The year is 2093 and the spaceship Prometheus has left Earth with scientists looking for the origins of life. Of course, their trip goes wrong. The special effects are terrific, as is the cast, particularly Noomi Rapace and Michael Fassbender, who steals the show.

Article adapted from *The Times*

Language note: review language

Reviews often use idioms or special terms to talk about films.

special effects = visual images made by computers

steal the show = get lots of attention

2 Read the reviews again and answer the questions.

1 Which film is not in English?
A Royal Affair

2 Which film is based on something that really happened?

....

3 Which actor plays the doctor in A Royal Affair?

....

4 What year is it in Prometheus?

....

5 Where does Prometheus take place?

....

6 Which actor does the writer like best in Prometheus?

....

3 Read the reviews again and underline the words and phrases that show that the writer liked the films.

4 Which film do you want to see?

I'd like to see .... because ....

....

5 What do these people do? Complete the sentences using words from the box.

actor	cast	director

1 The .... decides how the film should be made.

2 An .... plays a part in a film.

3 The .... is all the actors in a film.

B Checking film times online

1 You decide to go and see Prometheus and want to know if it's showing in 3D. Read the webpage on page 46 *very quickly* then tick the sentence that is true.

1 You can only watch Prometheus in 3D.

2 You can only watch Prometheus in 2D.

3 You can watch Prometheus in 2D and 3D.

Time	Booking	Home

A Royal Affair

Saturday	16:00	20:00	
Sunday	16:00	20:00	
Monday	*16:00*	20:00	

Prometheus 2D

Saturday	*10:00*	15:00	20:00
Sunday		15:00	20:00
Monday		15:00	20:00

Prometheus 3D

Saturday	10:00	16:00	20:20
Sunday		16:00	20:20
Monday	*14:20*	17:00	20:20

Film times in italics show special saver showings (all tickets £5)

Reading tip: looking for particular information

When reading for a particular piece of information, do *not* read every word. Pass your eyes over the text, looking just for the information you need. For example, if you are looking for the film times of a particular film, just scan the words until you find the title of the film you want to see, then read those times carefully.

2 Read the webpage again to find out which film time is best for you.

1 Today is Saturday. How many times is *Prometheus* in 3D shown today?

....

2 You are busy in the afternoon. What times can you watch *Prometheus* in 3D today?

.... / ....

3 Can you buy special saver tickets for *Prometheus* in 3D on Saturdays? If yes, what time does this showing start?

Yes / No ....

4 Can you buy special saver tickets for *Prometheus* in 2D on Saturdays? If yes, what time does this showing start?

Yes / No ....

C   Buying your ticket online

1   You buy your ticket online. Before you read, complete the sentences using the words in the box.

confirm	reserved	booking fee
quantity	purchase (noun)	total

1   The .... is the amount of several small amounts added together.

2   When you make a ...., you buy something.

3   We .... our seats yesterday because we were worried that there wouldn't be any left today.

4   Could you .... that the information on the ticket is correct?

5   The .... is the number of things that you are buying.

6   A .... is an extra amount of money that is sometimes added on when you buy tickets.

2   You are buying two special saver tickets for *Prometheus 2D,* on Saturday 11 November at 10:00. Read the webpage and circle the two mistakes.

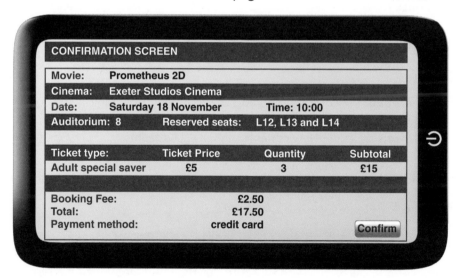

CONFIRMATION SCREEN

Movie:	Prometheus 2D	
Cinema:	Exeter Studios Cinema	
Date:	Saturday 18 November	Time: 10:00
Auditorium: 8	Reserved seats:	L12, L13 and L14

Ticket type:	Ticket Price	Quantity	Subtotal
Adult special saver	£5	3	£15

Booking Fee:	£2.50
Total:	£17.50
Payment method:	credit card

Confirm

My review

I can read a review to decide what film to see.	❑
I can find out particular information about a film and its showing times.	❑
I can make a purchase online.	❑

11 GETTING MEDICAL HELP

Getting started

1 Where do you go when you feel ill?
2 Why is it important to read information on medicine packets very carefully?
3 Is there anywhere else you can get medical help?

A Going to the doctor

1 You have just moved to Sydney, Australia and want to find out about the local medical centre. Before you read, match the words to the meanings.

1	surgery	a	an arrangement to see someone at a particular time
2	emergency	b	the person who is getting medical help
3	pharmacy	c	the place where you see a doctor
4	patient	d	a serious situation where you need help immediately
5	appointment	e	the place where you buy medicine

2 Read the leaflet *very quickly* then add the following headings in the correct places.

Appointments	New patients	Our team	Opening hours

Reading tip: using a dictionary

When you are reading, try to understand the main idea of the text without a dictionary. After reading, go back over the text and look up any new words. Did you need to understand these words to get the main idea of the text or could you guess what they meant?

3 Your son has been awake all night with an earache. It's now 7 am. Answer the questions.

1 Can you get him an appointment to see a doctor today? Yes / No

2 What do you need to do to get an appointment today?

....

South Quay Medical Centre

a ....

Dr Peter King

Dr Vicky Ho

Sister Kathy Steer

b ....

Morning surgery: 08:30–12:30   Afternoon surgery: 14:00–18:00

We are closed on Saturdays and Sundays, and on Thursday afternoons.

Outside our normal hours, call Sydney Out of Hours Medical Services on 02 3994 3993 for medical advice.

Late night pharmacies are also available – see www.sydneylatenightpharmacies.com

In a medical emergency, call 000.

c ....

Three types of appointments are available:

• appointments made in advance.

• same-day appointments. Call us by 08.30 as there are only a few available.

• emergency appointments are for people who need urgent help.

Home visits are only available for people who are unable to get to the surgery.

If you cannot keep an appointment, please let us know so that we can offer it to another patient.

d ....

To register, you must complete a health questionnaire and make an appointment for a health check with the nurse.

---

4 Read the leaflet again and answer the questions.

1 How many doctors are there at the South Quay Medical Centre?   Two

2 What is the nurse's name? ....

3 Can I make an appointment for Thursday at 4pm? ....

4 What time does morning surgery finish? ....

5 Who can have a home visit? ....

6 How do you register at the medical centre? ....

....

Reading tip: unknown words

When you see a new word, try to guess its meaning from the rest of the sentence. For example, if you don't know 'urgent' look at 'emergency' in the following sentence:

*Emergency appointments are for people who need **urgent** help.*

If you don't know what 'urgent' means, you can guess its meaning because you know what 'emergency' means. You can guess that in an emergency, you will need help immediately.

B ## Going to the pharmacy

1 Your son has earache so you go to the pharmacy to buy him some medicine. Before you read, choose the correct meaning of the words.

1 relief
  a something that makes pain better
  b something that makes pain worse

2 dosage
  a how much medicine you should take
  b the physical sign of a particular illness

3 overdose
  a when you take less medicine than the packet tells you
  b when you take more medicine than the packet tells you

4 side effects
  a pain down the side of your body
  b some other (usually bad) result of taking a medicine

5 symptom
  a how much medicine you should take
  b the physical sign of a particular illness

6 be allergic to something
  a be affected in a bad way by something
  b be told to take something by your doctor

Kidimed

Fast, effective relief
For 6+ years
Liquid

Contains paracetamol

Always read the enclosed leaflet carefully before use

2 Read the front of the box. What must you do *before* you give your son some medicine?

3 Read this leaflet from inside the medicine box. Are the sentences true or false? Write a ✓ in the correct place.

KIDIMED

INFORMATION LEAFLET

Fast, effective relief from:
• fever (high temperature)
• cold and flu symptoms
• toothache
• headache
• earache
• sore throat

Dosage:

Child's age	How much?
6–8 years	One 5ml spoonful
8–12 years	Two 5ml spoonfuls
12–16 years	Two to three 5ml spoonfuls

Do not give more than four doses in 24 hours.
Leave at least four hours between doses.
Do not give more than the recommended dose.
Each 5ml spoonful contains 250mg of paracetamol.

Possible side effects:
Side effects are very unlikely, but some children may experience:
• minor skin rashes
• mild stomach upsets

Do NOT give this to your child if they are:
• less than 6 years old
• allergic to Ibuprofen or aspirin

If symptoms continue for longer than three days, see your doctor.

If your child is taking any other medicine, see your doctor or pharmacist before using this product.

Keep out of the reach and sight of children. Check that the lid of the bottle is closed at all times.

Do not store above 25°C.

Contains paracetamol
Do not give this medicine with any other paracetamol-containing products.
Seek immediate medical attention in the event of an overdose.

	True	False
1 My son is ten years old, so he should take three 5ml spoonfuls of medicine.	....	✓
2 It's 4pm. He can have one dose now and another at 8pm.	....	....
3 Then I can give him doses every four hours, which means medicine at 12am, 4am, 8am, 12pm and 4pm over the next 24 hours.	....	....
4 My son might get a rash or a stomach upset after taking the medicine.	....	....
5 If he still has earache tomorrow, I should take him to the doctor.	....	....
6 My daughter is two years old. If she has earache, I can give her this medicine.	....	....

Language note: -ache words

We can sometimes add *-ache* to a body part to say that it is hurting.

headache   *toothache*   *earache*

My Review

I can understand information about a doctor's surgery.	❏
I can guess the meaning of a word from the rest of the sentence.	❏
I can read medicine packets carefully to understand how to take it safely.	❏

12 FLYING

Getting started

1 When did you last fly somewhere? Where did you go?
2 What information does this sign show?
3 What other information do you read at an airport?

A Checking in

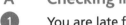

You are late for your flight to Canada. You must check in immediately, but there are very long queues. Read the notice *very quickly* then answer the questions.

1 Where can you check in quickly?

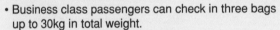

2 How much do you have to pay to check in quickly?

....

TRAVEL ADVICE

Baggage weight

- Economy class passengers can check in two bags up to 20kg in total weight.
- Business class passengers can check in three bags up to 30kg in total weight.
- Charge for overweight baggage: €50.
- Each passenger can take one piece of hand luggage on board the plane. This can weigh up to 7kg and must not be larger than 50 × 40 × 20cm.

FLY SAFE AIR

Check-in guidelines

- Passengers are NOT allowed to check in any dangerous materials. Please see separate notice for full list of prohibited items.
- Ensure that all checked-in bags are clearly labelled with your name, address, telephone number and email address.
- We recommend that you take valuables, important documents, money and medication in your hand luggage.
- Pack sharp objects in your checked-in bags and not your hand luggage.
- Pack liquids, gels or pastes in bottles larger than 100ml in your checked-in bags. You CANNOT take these through security in your hand luggage.

Fast-track check-in

- Please go to Check-in Desk 14A for fast-track check-in, which costs €10.

2 Match the words to the meanings.

1 passengers

2 baggage / luggage

3 weight

4 prohibited

5 valuables

a not allowed

b people travelling on the plane

c things that are worth a lot of money

d bags or suitcases

e how heavy something is

3 Your friend doesn't understand the notice. Read it again and answer his questions.

1 We're flying economy class, so how heavy can our checked-in bags be?
    Up to 20kg each.

2 Oh no, my bag's heavier than that. What will I have to pay?

    ....

3 And I've got two pieces of hand luggage, both 50 x 40 x 20cm. Is that OK?

    ....

4 I've got my passport and money in my hand luggage. Is that right?

    ....

5 Can I take my nail scissors in my hand luggage?

    ....

6 Can I pack my 200ml bottle of shower gel in my checked-in luggage?

    ....

B **Going through security**

1 What happens at security? Number the sentences in the correct order.

a Put the tray on the conveyor belt.   ......

b Collect your belongings from the security officer. ......

c Place your belongings in a tray.   ......

d Walk through the metal detector.   ......

2 Read the notice on page 54 *very quickly* then choose the best response.

1 It is about special offers in the airport shop – it's very important, so I will read it again carefully.

2 It is about what to do at security – it's not very important so I won't read it again.

3 It is about what to do at security – it's very important so I will read it again carefully.

SECURITY INFORMATION

Before you go through security, please:

• remove all coats and jackets, shoes and belts and place in a tray.

• place metallic items (mobile, coins, keys, etc.) from your pockets in a tray.

• remove laptops from cases and place them in a separate tray.

Any prohibited items will be taken by security.

At security:

• Place all your things on the conveyor belt.

• Walk through the metal detector. You may also be scanned by a handheld metal detector.

• Collect your items from the security officers.

Please note the following information about liquids:

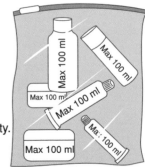

• All liquids, gels or pastes must be held in individual containers not exceeding 100ml.

• The containers must be carried in a separate, clear-plastic, zip-top or re-sealable bag, which must not be more than 20 × 20cm with a 1 litre capacity.

• Note that these restrictions may not apply to baby food and medicines.

 Security liquid restrictions are implemented by the Department for Transport. Information is correct August 2012.

Reading tip: headings and bullet points

Headings and bullet points can help you find what you are looking for quickly. For example, if you want to find out more about security restrictions on liquids, read the headings until you find one that contains 'liquids', then check the bullet points to find the information you need.

---

3 Your friend wants to check that he has understood the notice correctly. Are his statements true or false? Correct any that are false.

1 I must take off my coat and put it on the conveyor belt.

True

2 I must keep my shoes on.

....

3 I must empty my pockets, put my things in a tray and put the tray on the conveyor belt.

....

4 I can take my 90ml bottle of shampoo in a clear, re-sealable plastic bag.

....

5   I can take my 1litre bottle of water in a clear, re-sealable plastic bag.

....

6   I may be able take my 150ml bottle of medicine in a clear, re-sealable plastic bag.

....

Reading tip: airport security notices

Always read airport security notices very carefully. The rules for air travel change all the time, so you need to know exactly what you can and can't take on a plane.

C   Boarding the plane

1 It's nearly time for your plane to leave. Check your boarding pass and answer the questions.

1   What's my flight number?

....

2   What gate do I need to go to?

....

3   What time do I need to get to the gate?

....

4   What's my seat number?

....

BOARDING PASS			**BOARDING PASS**
Passenger name: JOHNS, ALEXANDER			Passenger name: JOHNS, ALEXANDER
			From: BARCELONA
From: BARCELONA	Date: 16 MAY	Flight: CAF923	To: VANCOUVER
To: VANCOUVER	Time: 10:40		Flight: CAF923 Date: 16 MAY
FLY SAFE AIR			Time: 10:40 Seat: 37C
			Boarding from GATE 19 at 09:55

My review

I can understand information at the check-in desk.	❏
I can read what you can and can't take through security.	❏
I can find information on a boarding pass.	❏

13 CATCHING A TRAIN

Getting started

1 What cities do you often visit or catch a train from?
2 Do you usually use buses or trains for long journeys?
3 What information do you read at the station or on a train?

A Checking train information online

1 You want to travel from London to Birmingham, so you check the train information online. Before you read, match the words to the meanings.

1	departure	a	details about the journey
2	arrival	b	when the train leaves
3	duration	c	when the train arrives
4	changes	d	how long the journey takes
5	information	e	how many times you change trains

2 Read the webpage and answer the questions on the opposite page.

Choose train times & fares

London (All stations) › Birmingham (All stations)

1st First class Fares	FROM £16.00	🔔 Set up journey alerts					Buy cheapest for £6.00

Wed 09 May

Other cheap fares

⬆ Earlier trains

Single from **£6.00**
Based on 1 adult

Dep.	From	To	Arr.	Dur.	Chg.		Status	
09:43	London Euston (EUS)	Birmingham New Street (BHM) Platform 6	11:08	1h25m	0	ℹ	✔	○ **£39.00** First Class Advance More fares
09:46	London Euston (EUS)	Birmingham New Street (BHM) Platform 3A	12:01	2h15m	0	ℹ	✔	CHEAPEST FARE ○ **£6.00** Advance More fares
10:03	London Euston (EUS)	Birmingham New Street (BHM) Platform 2	11:27	1h24m	0	ℹ	✔	○ **£20.00** Advance More fares
10:07	London Marylebone (MYB) Platform 2	Birmingham Snow Hill (BSW) Platform 2	11:59	1h25m	0	ℹ	✔	○ **£15.00** Advance More fares

⬇ Later trains

1   How much is the cheapest ticket to Birmingham?

   ....

2   What time does this train leave and what time does it arrive?

   ....

3   What London station does it leave from and what Birmingham station does it go to?

   ....

4   Do you have to change trains?

   ....

5   Which is the fastest train to Birmingham and how much does it cost?

   ....

Language note: abbreviations

These abbreviations are often used on timetables:

- Dep. = Departure
- Arr. = Arrival
- Dur. = Duration
- Chg. = Change
- Info = Information

B   Understanding notices at a station

1   You plan to return to London tomorrow and see a notice on the platform. Read it very quickly and answer the questions.

1   Is it important information about your train journey tomorrow?

   ....

2   Do you need to read it again carefully?

   ....

CUSTOMER INFORMATION

Start date: 9 May   **End date: 10 May**

Routes affected: Birmingham New Street to Coventry and Birmingham New Street to Euston

- Buses will replace trains, leaving from Birmingham New Street at 05, 25 and 45 past each hour and go to Coventry.
- Journey times may be extended by up to 50 minutes.
- For passengers travelling between Birmingham New Street and London Euston, journey times may be extended by 20 minutes.
- Trains from Birmingham New Street will depart a few minutes earlier than scheduled.

To get options for your journey, please use the National Rail Enquiries real-time Journey Planner.

---

2 Read the notice again carefully. Are the sentences true or false? Write a ✓ in the correct place.

	True	False
1 Trains to and from London Euston will not be delayed.	....	....
2 Buses will replace trains between London Euston and Birmingham New Street.	....	....
3 There will be three buses every hour from Birmingham New Street to Coventry.	....	....
4 The journey between London Euston and Birmingham New Street will take 20 minutes longer than usual.	....	....
5 Trains for London Euston will leave from Birmingham New Street on time.	....	....

Reading tip: long notices

Do not ignore long notices because they might be important. Skim or scan them first to see what sort of information they contain and then read them carefully if they are relevant to your journey.

C   Understanding signs on a train

1   You see these signs on the train. What do they mean? Read the signs and choose the best answer.

Do not leave luggage unattended at any time.

1 a Remember to take your bags with you when you leave the train.

b Always stay with your bags.

c Leave your bags here.

THIS WC IS OUT OF ORDER.
Please use alternative facilities in Carriage 3.

2 a You can't use this toilet. There is another one in Coach C.

b You can't use this toilet and there aren't any other toilets on the train.

c You can use this toilet or you can use the toilet in Coach C.

ALARM
Emergency use only to talk with driver

3 a You can speak to the driver if you want to.

b You can speak to the driver in an emergency.

c You can't speak to the driver.

TRAIN TICKET

You must buy a ticket before you get on one of our trains.

4 a You should buy your ticket on the train.

b You should buy your ticket before you leave London.

c You should buy your ticket when you arrive in Birmingham.

2 Find words in the signs that mean:

1 suitcases / bags   l ....

2 not looked after   u ....

3 toilet   W ....

4 another / different   a ....

5 not working / broken   o ....

6 something that makes a loud noise to warn of danger   a ....

My review

I can find out times and prices of trains online.	☐
I can read a notice quickly to find out if it's important.	☐
I can understand station notices and train signs.	☐

14 TAKING A BUS

Getting started

1 How often do you take a bus?

2 Where do you travel by bus?

3 What information do you think this person is reading?

A Finding out about the next bus

1 You are waiting for a bus and check the app on your phone to see when it will come. Before you read, complete the sentences using the words in the box.

on time	delayed	due	cancelled

1 The M3 bus will not run – it's been ....

2 The R12 bus will not be early or late – it's ....

3 The M1 bus is running late – it's been .... by five minutes but is .... any time now.

2 Read the app *very quickly* then circle the correct answer.

1 The next M7 bus is due in *4 / 14 / 15* minutes.

2 There *aren't any / are some* delays on Route 7 today.

3 There *aren't any / are some* delays on other bus routes today.

02-UK 3G   3:56 PM

Routes		★
Last Updated 15:57		
Route M8	Olympic Village	Due >
Route R14	Powell	4 mins >
Route M7	Yaletown	Cancelled >
Route R14	Powell	8 mins >
Route M7	Yaletown	14 mins >
Route M8	Olympic Village	15 mins >
Route R14		

Alert: Some delays and cancellations to Route 7 due to emergency roadworks in Granville.
All other services running on time.

Settings	

3 Other people at the bus stop notice you are using this app. Answer their questions.

1 When's the next M8 bus coming?

It's due now.

2 When's the next bus to Powell due?

....

3 What bus do I need to get to Yaletown?

....

4 Why are there problems with Route 7?

....

5 Is the bus for the Olympic Village leaving soon?

....

B Understanding notices at the bus stop

1 While you are waiting for the bus, you see a notice (see page 62). Before you read it, choose the correct meaning of these words.

1 fare

   a how long your bus journey takes

   b the money you pay to travel on a bus

2 increase

   a get larger

   b get smaller

3 peak

   a the most expensive time to travel

   b the cheapest time to travel

4 off-peak

   a the most expensive time to travel

   b the cheapest time to travel

5 concession

   a a cheaper ticket for a particular group of people

   b a more expensive ticket for a particular group of people

2 Read the notice on page 62 *very quickly*. What is it about?

1 Ticket prices

2 Changes to some bus routes

3 New ticket machines

FARES INCREASE NOTICE

Please note that from 1 January, there will be increases in some fares.

SINGLE PEAK-RATE* FARES

Zones crossed	Adult	Concession
1	$3.00	$1.75
2	$4.00	$2.70
3	$5.00	$3.00

Please note that single off-peak and 7-day supersaver fares will stay the same price.

Remember that if you are buying your ticket on the bus, you must have the exact change. You can also buy tickets before getting on the bus at our ticket machines, which give change.

* Peak rate applies on weekdays from 7am to 7pm. Off-peak ticket prices are unchanged.

** In Vancouver, there are three bus zones. The amount you pay depends on the number of zones that you cross on your journey.

*** Concession fares are for children aged 5 to 15, seniors over 65 with proof of age and students with valid student ID cards. Children under 5 go free.

---

3 Are the sentences true or false? Correct any that are false.

1 It's 4 January, so the ticket prices have not gone up yet.

False. Ticket prices go up on 1 January.

2 The only ticket prices that have changed are single off-peak fares.

....

3 There are three bus zones in Vancouver.

....

4 A 25-year-old travelling across three zones at 3pm will have to pay $5.

....

5 A 67-year-old travelling across two zones at 10am will have to pay $1.75.

....

6 A 16-year-old student, without student ID, travelling across one zone at 4pm will have to pay $1.75.

....

4 Complete the sentences using the prepositions in the box.

on	to	for	in	on

1 There has been an increase .... the number of passengers.

2 You can pay .... your ticket at a ticket machine.

3 You can also pay when you get .... the bus.

4 The fare you pay depends .... how far you travel.

5 Children aged 5 .... 15 pay less.

Reading tip: what does * mean?

If you see a * (called 'an asterisk') in a text, then it means that there is a note at the bottom giving you more information. If there is more than one note, then two ** (or more) are used.

C Reading signs on the bus

1 You see these signs on the bus. Match the signs to the meanings.

1

a Please offer this seat to someone who needs it more than you do.

2

b No smoking.

3

c Please don't play your music too loudly.

4

d Emergency door. In case of emergency only, turn handle.

My review

I can check when the next bus is coming on an app.	☐
I can read notices about bus fares.	☐
I can understand what signs on buses mean.	☐

15 TRAVELLING BY CAR

Getting started

1 How often do you travel by car?

2 What do you read when you travel by car?

3 Do you use technology when you travel by car?

A   Following directions

1   You are driving from Chicago International Airport to Lincoln Park. You check the directions online. Read the directions *very quickly* and answer the question.

How long does it take to get to Lincoln Park?

a   15.6 minutes

b   26 minutes

c   11 minutes

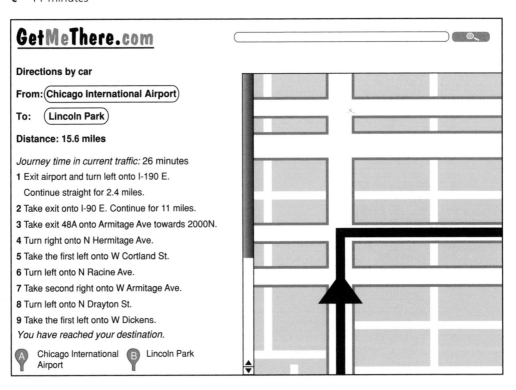

GetMeThere.com

Directions by car

From: Chicago International Airport

To: Lincoln Park

Distance: 15.6 miles

Journey time in current traffic: 26 minutes

1 Exit airport and turn left onto I-190 E.
 Continue straight for 2.4 miles.

2 Take exit onto I-90 E. Continue for 11 miles.

3 Take exit 48A onto Armitage Ave towards 2000N.

4 Turn right onto N Hermitage Ave.

5 Take the first left onto W Cortland St.

6 Turn left onto N Racine Ave.

7 Take second right onto W Armitage Ave.

8 Turn left onto N Drayton St.

9 Take the first left onto W Dickens.

You have reached your destination.

Ⓐ Chicago International   Ⓑ Lincoln Park
  Airport

2   Match the words to the meanings.

1	directions	**a**	the place you are going to
2	destination	**b**	instructions that tell you how to get to a place
3	distance	**c**	when you go from one place to another
4	journey	**d**	the amount of space between two places

Reading tip: directions

Always read through directions carefully before you begin your journey to make sure that you understand exactly what they say. Use a map as well to help you to understand the text. The abbreviations N, E, S, W are often used for the compass points.

---

3   Read the directions again and answer the driver's questions.

1   Lincoln Park is 26 miles away from Chicago International Airport, isn't it?
No, it isn't. It's 15.6 miles away from the airport.

2   I turn left when I get out of the airport, don't I?

....

3   OK, we're on the I-90 E. I need to stay on this road for 11 miles, don't I?

....

4   OK, so we're on W. Cortland Street and I need to turn left onto N. Racine Avenue, don't I?

....

5   And then I need to take exit 48C for Armitage Avenue towards 2000W, don't I?

....

6   OK, we're on North Drayton Street now. I need to take the second left onto West Dickens, don't I?

....

Language note: compass points

N = North

E = East

S = South

W = West

B **Understanding road signs**

1 As you drive, you see these road signs. Before you read, complete the sentences using the words in the box.

detour	priority	required	resident

1 If you have ...., it means that you can go first.

2 If you are a ...., it means you live in that place.

3 A .... is a different route that traffic must take when the road is closed.

4 If something is ...., it means that it is needed.

2 What do these signs mean? Choose the best answer.

1

a Continue driving and you will see people working on the road.

b You cannot continue driving because people are working on the road. You must follow the arrow.

c Follow the arrow and you will see people working on the road.

2

a You cannot pass – this road is closed at the end.

b You can pass – this road is open at the end.

c You can pass – this road is closed at the end.

3

a You can go before vehicles coming the other way.

b You must let vehicles coming the other way go first.

c You must go at the same time as the vehicles coming the other way.

3 When you get to Lincoln Park, you look for somewhere to park. Read the signs and choose the best endings for the sentences.

1

You can ...

a sometimes leave your car here.

b never leave your car here.

2 If you live in this apartment, …

    a you can park here.

    b you cannot park here.

3 If you are visiting somebody who lives in this apartment, …

    a you can park in the visitors' parking area.

    b you can park here.

RESIDENT PARKING ONLY.

VISITORS MUST PARK ONLY IN VISITORS' PARKING AREA.

4 I want to stay for 90 minutes, so I must pay …

    a $2.00

    b $3.00

5 I use a wheelchair so I pay …

    a $2.00.

    b nothing.

6 I drive a motorbike …

    a so I can park here if I pay.

    b so I can't park here.

7 It's 10 p.m. on a Sunday …

    a so I have to pay.

    b so I don't have to pay.

PARKING METER TARIFF
Enforced hours 9am–9pm every day
Up to 1 hour $1.00
Up to 2 hours $2.00
Up to 4 hours $3.00
Free for disabled persons
No motorcycles

My review

I can follow directions to get to a destination. ☐

I can understand road signs. ☐

I can read parking notices. ☐

16 TRAVELLING ON FOOT

Getting started

1 Do you enjoy going for walks?
2 If so, where do you like to go for a walk?
3 What do you read when you walk?

A Using an app

1 You go for a walk. You download an app to use while you are walking. Before you read, match the words to the meanings.

1	distance	**a**	how quickly something moves
2	speed	**b**	happening now
3	calories	**c**	the amount of space between two places
4	current	**d**	calculated by adding amounts together and then dividing by the number of amounts
5	average	**e**	a way of measuring the energy value of food

2 Read the app *very quickly* and choose the best description.

1 It shows me the route of my walk on a map and tells me what I will see as I walk.
2 It tracks my walk on a map and tells me how far and how fast I've walked.
3 It shows me the quickest route and gives me directions.

3 Read the app again and answer the questions.

1 How far have you walked? ....

2 How long has that taken you? ....

3 How fast are you going at the moment? ....

4 What is your average speed? ....

5 How many calories have you burnt? ....

Reading tip: reading apps

There are now millions of apps available for most kinds of phone. Apps are useful because they let you practise your English reading when you are on the move, or whenever you have a minute or two to spare.

B   Understanding signs and notices

1 As you walk you see these signs and notices. Before you read, complete the sentences using the words in the box.

private	hazard	beware of	pedestrian	access	accompanied by

1 A .... is a person who is walking.

2 If something is ...., then it belongs to one person and not to everyone.

3 If you're .... somebody, then you go somewhere with that person.

4 .... is another word for danger.

5 If you have .... to a place, then you are allowed to go there.

6 If you tell somebody to .... something, then you are warning them that something might be dangerous.

2 Read the signs on page 70 *very quickly*. What are they about?

1 Signs warning you of danger 1 ....

2 Signs telling you that you are not allowed somewhere ....

3 Signs helping you to cross safely ....

1 DANGER! ELECTRICAL HAZARD

2 No pedestrian access

3 Beware of the dog

4 Keep out Private property

5 Bike lane Look both ways

6 Pedestrians Push button and wait for walk signal

3 Read the signs again and choose the best answer.

1 If you see sign 1, will you:

    a stay away?   **b** get nearer?

2 If you see sign 2, will you:

    a keep walking?   **b** find another way to walk?

3 If you see sign 3, will you:

    a be careful to avoid the dog?   **b** say hello to the dog and stroke it?

4 If you see sign 4, will you:

    a open the gate and keep walking?   **b** find another way to walk?

5 If you see sign 5, will you:

    a keep walking?

    b look left and right to make sure no bikes are coming before continuing?

6 If you see sign 6, will you:

    a press the button and wait for the signal before walking?

    b press the button and then walk on straight away?

4 As you walk, you see this notice. You are with your dog and want to go through Langmans Park. Read the notice *very quickly* and choose the best answer.

1 I can't take my dog into Langmans Park.

2 I can take my dog into Langmans Park but must keep it on a lead.

3 I can take my dog into Langmans Park and let it run free.

Langmans Park RULES AND REGULATIONS

1- Opening hours: 6am to 11pm.
2- Fires must only be lit in the barbecue grills. No open fires.
3- Children under 12 must be accompanied by an adult.
4- Skateboards, roller blades, and bicycles only allowed on walkways.
5- No ball games except in basketball and tennis court areas.
6- Dogs must be kept on a lead and kept under control at all times.
7- Pet owners must clear up pet waste and put it in the designated bins.

Fines of up to $500 if you do not follow the rules and regulations of the park.

5 Read the notice again. Are the sentences true or false? Write a ✓ in the correct place.

	True ✓	False
1 You can have a barbecue in the park.	....	....
2 A 6-year-old can only come into the park with an adult.	....	....
3 A 13-year-old can only come into the park with an adult.	....	....
4 You must not ride your bike in the park.	....	....
5 You can play ball games in some parts of the park.	....	....
6 If you do not follow the rules, you might have to pay $1000.	....	....

Language note: must/mustn't

In rules and regulations, we use:

• must + verb to say what you have to do.
• mustn't + verb to say what you can't do.

My review

I can read an app on my walk.	❑
I can understand short signs on my walk.	❑
I can understand long notices on my walk.	❑

17 NEWSPAPERS

Getting started

1 Why do people read newspapers?
2 How often do you read a newspaper?
3 What's your favourite newspaper?

A Reading headlines

1 Read the headlines and choose what each article is about.

US President to visit China

a The US President visited China today.

b The US President will visit China.

Roadside bomb kills 14

a 14 people were killed by a bomb.

b 14 bombs exploded today, killing some people.

E-reader revolution for Africa

a There's been a big change in politics in Africa.

b There's been a big change in education in Africa.

Language note: headlines

The grammar used in headlines is different from standard written English:

- Articles are not always used.
- A string of nouns may be used so you have to work out what the verb might be.
- The infinitive is used to refer to the future.

B   Reading newspaper articles

1 One of the headlines from exercise A1 fits the article below. Read it *very quickly* then add the headline.

....

Schools in developing countries try digital books

By Geoffrey A. Fowler & Nicholas Bariyo

It is time for a vocabulary lesson in Bernard Opio's sixth-form class at the Humble Primary School in Mukono, Uganda. One new word the students have already learned this year is 'e-reader'. Mr. Opio tells them to get out their e-readers. Within seconds, most of the students have a digital dictionary open on their screens.

10 'It took the kids just a few days to learn how to use **them**,' says Mr. Opio. 'Instead of just having 1,000 books, they have 10 times or 100 times **that**,' says David Risher, from the non-profit organization Worldreader that is trying out e-readers in some schools in Uganda and two other African countries.

19 Mr Risher, 46, has raised about $1.5 million for his two-year-old program, which has given 1,100 e-readers and 180,000 e-books to kids and teachers in Ghana, Kenya, and Uganda. Early results are good, says Mr Risher – in Worldreader's first test, they found that primary-school students who got e-readers improved **their** reading on tests from about 13% to 16%.

29 E-readers have some advantages. They are light and hard-wearing, and can last weeks on a single charge. With built-in Internet connections, **they** are like big

mobile phones. And it is easy to publish the work of local authors digitally on e-readers. Before, Humble School's library had books sent from America. 'The first books we got were about the US, with kids playing in ice, which our children would not understand,' says Ester Nabwire, the school's head teacher. 'With the e-readers, there are African authors, African names which are exciting the kids.'

44 E-readers are still quite expensive. Getting an e-book into the hands of one of Worldreader's kids costs about $5 per title. **That** includes the $100 price of the e-reader, a case, and other costs. Worldreader gets e-books that are available for free or given by publishers, or by digitally publishing work by local authors.

53 For kids who start to love reading, there is another advantage: a very large library. 'I can get every book I want to read very quickly,' says Eperence Uwera, a 13-year-old Rwandan refugee at the Humble School. 'I would love to go [home] with the e-reader during the holidays.'

Article adapted from *The Wall Street Journal*

2 Match the beginnings and ends of the phrases.

1 developing   **a** publish

2 non-profit   **b** Internet connection

3 built-in   **c** countries

4 digitally   **d** organization

3 Complete the sentences using the phrases from Exercise 2.

1 If a phone has a ...., you can use it to go online.

2 .... do not have high levels of industry or business, and many people living there have low incomes.

3 When you .... a book, you make it available to readers online.

4 A .... uses money that it makes to try to achieve its aims.

4 Read the article again and choose the best summary.

1 The program sends used books to students in Africa to help improve their reading.

2 The program gives children in Africa e-readers instead of traditional books to help improve their reading.

3 The program sends teachers to primary schools in Africa to help improve children's reading.

5 Are the sentences true or false? Correct any that are false.

1 The students at Humble Primary School learnt how to use their new e-readers quickly.
True.

2 The Worldreader program has been running for 3 years.

....

3 They have given e-readers to students in Ghana, Kenya, and Uganda.

....

4 They still don't know if e-readers are helping students to improve their reading.

....

5 Este Nabwire says that African children prefer reading stories written for American children.

....

6 It costs about $5 per title to get e-readers to African children.

....

6 Read the article again and find three advantages of using e-readers.

1 ....

2 ....

3 ....

Reading tip: English-language news online

If you find English-language news difficult to understand, try reading a news story in your own language first so that you already know what it's about. Then go to an English-language news website and find the same story.

---

7 Look at the bold words in the article and choose the best answer.

1 'them' in line 11 refers to:

   a the e-readers

   b the students

2 'that' in line 13 refers to:

   a 1,000 e-readers

   b 1,000 books

3 'their' in line 27 refers to:

   a the students'

   b the teachers'

4 'they' in line 32 refers to:

   a the advantages of e-readers

   b the e-readers

5 'that' in line 47 refers to:

   a getting an e-book into the hands of a Worldreader child

   b the price of $5

My review

I can understand headlines. ❏

I can read newspaper articles. ❏

I can decide which is the best summary of a newspaper article. ❏

I can understand references such as 'that' and 'they' in a text. ❏

18 MAGAZINES

Getting started

1 Why do you think people read magazines?
2 What are your favourite magazines?
3 How often do you read them?

A Reading headlines and straplines

1 Read the headline and strapline, and answer the questions.

Up close with ... MESSI

*Read Jason Cowley's rare interview with Lionel Messi, the **world's best footballer***

1 What do you think the article is about?

   a Jason Cowley, who doesn't give interviews very often.

   b How Messi compares with other footballers in the world.

   c An interview that Jason Cowley did with Messi.

2 What does 'up close' mean in the headline?

   a Cowley is 'up close' to Messi because he played football against him.

   b Cowley is 'up close' to Messi because he is the world's best footballer.

   c Cowley is 'up close' to Messi because he interviewed him face-to-face.

3 Who doesn't give interviews very often?

   a Jason Cowley

   b Messi

Reading tip: topic sentences

Often, the first sentence of a paragraph summarizes the rest of that paragraph. This is very useful when you are reading quickly because sometimes you can just read the first line of each paragraph to get the general idea of what the text is about.

B   Reading magazine articles

1   Read the article *very quickly* then choose the best topic sentence (1–5) for each paragraph (a–e).

1   He earns a lot of money.

2   Everything Messi does in public is controlled.

3   So, overall, how does it feel being Lionel Messi, to know that you are the best football player in the world?

4   How can I describe the brilliance of Messi, who is not only the world's best footballer, but perhaps the best ever to play the game?

5   His life has been unusual.

---

a ...

Thierry Henry, a former team-mate at FC Barcelona, thinks that the best thing is not to talk about Messi, but to watch him.

Football is a game. I'm trying to have fun. The day I stop having fun is the day I retire.

Simon Kuper, in his book *The Football Men*, calls Messi the classic Argentine *pibe*, the man-boy who is still like a child. In other words, football for him is play. 'So are you the classic *pibe*?' I ask Messi. 'That's what I'm trying to do,' he says. 'Football is a game. I'm trying to have fun. The day I stop having fun is the day I retire.'

b ...

I was told Messi earns £32 million a year. However, there's something attractively modest about him. He lives cleanly and quietly in Spain with his family and his Argentine girlfriend – his childhood sweetheart, Antonella Roccuzzo.

c ...

I ask him if it feels as though he is living in a golden prison, from which he escapes only to play football. 'I try to live as normal a life as I can,' he says. 'I try to go to the cinema, to shop in the centre, to go out to a restaurant. Fortunately in the city of Barcelona, people allow me to live as a normal person, like I am.'

d ...

Born on June 24, 1987 in Santa Fe, Argentina, Lionel Messi arrived with his father in Barcelona when he was 13. Although he was suffering from a growth hormone deficiency, he was very determined and FC Barcelona thought he was good enough to join them. Now he is considered to be their best player.

I believe better things will come. I have so much to learn. Remember: I am only 24 years old.

e ...

Such a question Messi says is 'very complicated'. He prefers to play than to think about such questions. 'I am very grateful for everything I've been able to achieve, for the family I have, for the people around me. But I believe better things will come. I have so much to learn. Remember: I am only 24 years old.'

Article adapted from *The Times Magazine*. © Jason Cowley/ The Times/ NI Syndication

2 Look again at the words in bold and choose the most likely meaning from their context.

1 How can I describe the **brilliance** of Messi, who is not only the world's best footballer, but perhaps the best ever to play the game?

    a greatness

    b weakness

2 'The day I stop having fun is the day I **retire**.'

    a stop working

    b work harder

3 I was told Messi earns £32 million a year. However, there's something attractively **modest** about him. He lives cleanly and quietly in Spain ...

    a humble and moderate

    b proud and arrogant

4 Everything Messi does **in public** is controlled.

    a away from other people

    b in front of other people

5 'I am very grateful for everything I've been able to **achieve**'

    a do successfully

    b do unsuccessfully

3 Read the interview again and answer the questions.

1 How does Simon Kuper describe Messi?

He describes him as the classic Argentine pibe, the man-boy who is still like a child.

2 How does Messi describe football and why he plays it?

....

3 What's Messi's salary?

....

4 What's his girlfriend's name?

....

5 Where was he born?

....

6 How old was he when he went to Barcelona?

....

4 How does the writer feel about Messi? Match the beginnings to the ends of the sentences.

1 He admires Messi's footballing skills ...

a because he says that, 'there is something attractively modest about Messi'.

2 He likes the fact that Messi lives a moderate, humble life ...

b because he says that he was 'determined' and kept on trying to achieve his goal in spite of a growth hormone deficiency.

3 He thinks Messi is very motivated to succeed ...

c because he says that, 'he is not only the world's best footballer, but perhaps the best ever to play the game'.

Language note: new speaker, new line

Remember when reading interviews in magazines that each new speaker starts on a new line. This will help you to keep track of who is saying what.

---

5 The writer uses signposting language to link phrases and sentences together. Match the words in bold to the explanations a–c.

a To show a contrast or balance (synonym: 'even though')
b To make a final point (synonym: 'to sum up')
c To explain a point in a different way (synonym: 'to put it simply')

1 'Simon Kuper, in his book *The Football Men*, calls Messi the classic Argentine *pibe*, the man-boy who is still like a child. **In other words**, football for him is play.'   ....

2 '**Although** he was suffering from a growth hormone deficiency, he was very determined.'   ....

3 'So, **overall**, how does it feel being Lionel Messi?'   ....

My review

I can understand headlines and straplines.   ☐
I can guess unknown words from their context.   ☐
I can understand how an interviewer feels about the person they are interviewing.   ☐
I can understand signposting language in a text.   ☐

19 MUSIC AND TV

Getting started

1 What do you think this person is doing?

2 How do you find out about new music? How do you buy new music?

3 How do you find out what is on TV?

A Finding out about new music

1 Read the website *very quickly* then choose the best description.

a This is a music streaming website where you can listen to, and share, tracks.

b This is a website providing news about the music industry.

c This is a music download site where you can buy new music.

2   **What links should these people click on to find out more?**

1   I'd love to see Sozzy Oz live.
Sozzy Oz announces new tour dates

2   I've heard that they're going to release a new version of *Good Grace*.

....

3   I follow the charts and always download the week's biggest selling single.

....

4   I'd like to find out about a Power Phone.

....

5   I want to watch some music videos.

....

6   The Fargo Festival was great! I wonder if there are any pictures online.

....

3   **Match the beginnings to the ends of the idioms.**

1	in	**a**	the cards
2	out	**b**	a flash
3	for	**c**	good
4	on	**d**	for grabs
5	up	**e**	of the question

4   **Write the idioms from Exercise 3 next to the correct meanings.**

1   very quickly   ....

2   available   ....

3   permanently, forever   ....

4   likely to happen   ....

5   impossible   ....

Reading tip: song lyrics

Reading song lyrics is a great way to practise your reading and improve your vocabulary. Find your favourite song lyrics online and read them while listening to the song.

B   Choosing what to watch on TV

1 Choose each person's favourite type of TV programme from the box.

| comedy   DIY programmes   cookery programmes   nature documentaries   reality TV |

1 I love cooking and am always looking for new ideas. ....

2 I really enjoy funny TV shows that make me laugh. ....

3 I like TV shows that tell real stories about real people. ....

4 I really enjoy programmes about animals and wildlife. ....

5 I want some ideas about home improvements. ....

2 Look at the TV listings *very quickly*. It is 7.30pm and you're watching ITV2. What programme is on?

....

Channel	7pm		8pm	9pm
BBC1	The One Show	Eastenders	DIY SOS	National Lottery Show
BBC2	Live Athletics			
ITV1	Emmerdale	Coronation Street	Batman Begins 🎬	
Channel 4	The Channel 4 News		Come Dine With Me	24 Hours in A & E
Channel 5	Marco Pierre White's Kitchen Wars		Building the London Underground	Big Brother
BBC3	Doctor Who		Shrek 🎬	
BBC4	Wonders of the Solar System		Legends: Roy Orbison in England	
ITV2	America's Got Talent		You've Been Framed	Gladiator 🎬
ITV3	Murder She Wrote		Agatha Christie's Poirot	Ronnie Corbett's Comedy Britain
ITV4	Tour de France Cycle Race Highlights		The Incredible Hulk 🎬	

Language note: shortened forms

Have you seen these shortened forms?

DIY	Do-It-Yourself
SOS	Help
A&E	Accident & Emergency (department in a hospital)

---

3 Answer the questions.

1 You want to watch a film. What films are on this evening?

....

....

....

....

2 You want to watch some sport. What sport programmes are on this evening?

....

....

3 You are interested in home improvements. What should you watch tonight?

Programme: .... Channel: .... Time: ....

4 You want to watch Agatha Christie's *Poirot*. What channel is it on and at what time?

Channel: .... Time: ....

5 You love Roy Orbison's music. What should you watch tonight?

Programme: .... Channel: .... Time: ....

6 What's on Channel 5 at 9pm?

....

4 It's 8pm and you want to decide what to watch. Fill in the blanks.

I would watch .... because I like ....

My review

I can find out about new music from a music website.	❑
I can choose what to watch on TV by reading TV listings.	❑
I can understand some shortened forms of English.	❑

20 FOLLOWING INSTRUCTIONS

Getting started

1 What is this person reading?

2 Do you always read the instructions when you buy something new?

3 Do you usually find instructions easy to follow?

A Following step-by-step instructions

1 Read the instructions below for a digital camera *very quickly*, then choose the best description.

a How to make a movie on the camera.

b How to take photographs on the camera.

c How to transfer photographs from the camera to the computer.

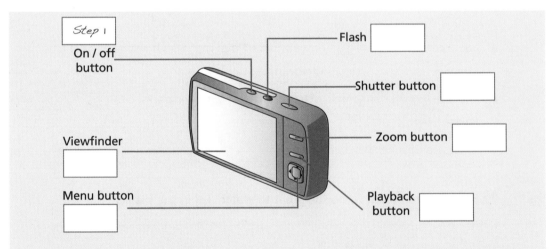

Step 1

On / off button

Flash

Shutter button

Viewfinder

Zoom button

Menu button

Playback button

1 Press the on / off button to turn on the camera.

2 Aim the camera towards the subject until you can see the photograph in the viewfinder. Be careful not to cover the flash with your fingers.

3 Zoom in or out using the zoom button until you are happy with the photograph.

4 Press the shutter button halfway down until the camera focuses on the subject of the photograph.

5 Press the shutter button all the way down and hold it for a moment to take the picture. Keep the camera as still as you can during this part of the process.

6 Press the playback button to view the photograph.

Reading tip: step-by-step instructions

When reading instructions, start by reading them quickly all the way to the end to get an idea of what you have to do. Then read each step carefully. Also, look closely at the pictures because they can help you understand difficult words.

2 Match the verbs to the meanings.

1	press	**a**	make a photograph clearer by adjusting the camera lens
2	cover	**b**	point the camera at the thing you want to take a picture of
3	zoom in / out	**c**	look at
4	aim	**d**	place something over something else
5	focus	**e**	adjust the camera lens for a close-up picture / long shot
6	view	**f**	push (a button) to make it work

3 Read the instructions again. Are the sentences true or false? Correct any that are false.

1 The first thing you need to do is aim the camera towards what you want to take a picture of.

False. The first thing you need to do is turn the camera on.

2 When taking a photograph, you must be careful not to cover the viewfinder with your fingers.

....

3 When you are happy with the photograph in the viewfinder, you should press the shutter button all the way down to focus on the subject of the photograph.

....

4 It's important to keep the camera still when you press the button all the way down to take the picture.

....

5 If you want to see the photograph after you have taken it, you should press the menu button.

....

4 Look at the picture of the camera. When do you use each button? Write the number in the boxes to show the order you will use them in (two boxes share the same step).

B   Troubleshooting

1 What does 'troubleshooting' mean? Choose the best definition.

1 Fixing problems   **2** Making problems   **3** Avoiding problems

2 Read the Troubleshooting page *very quickly* and write the headings in the correct places.

1 I can't take a picture with my camera.

2 The viewfinder has gone blank.

3 I can't switch my camera on.

TROUBLESHOOTING

a ....

› Make sure that the batteries are fully charged – see 'Charging the batteries' (page 7).

› Check that the batteries are installed correctly – see 'Installing the batteries' (page 8).

b ....

› The batteries sometimes don't work in low temperatures. Take them out of the camera and warm them in your pocket, then try turning your camera on again.

› Ensure that the camera is not set to playback mode – see 'Using playback' (page 14).

› Make sure that the memory card is in the camera. Check also that it isn't full. If it is, then download the photographs to your computer and delete some.

c ....

› If your camera's power saving mode is enabled, then it will make the viewfinder go blank after a set period of inactivity – see 'Enabling the power saving mode' (page 18).

› It's possible that the camera is locked. To reset the camera, remove the batteries and memory card and wait for at least five minutes before reinserting them and restarting it.

– 4 –

Language note: 're' at the start of words

When we put 're' at the start of a word, for example, 'reinserting' and 'restarting', it means that we are doing those things again.

*I tried to **insert** the batteries in the camera but they were the wrong way around. So I took them out and **reinserted** them.*

*I started to take photos but the memory card was full. So I downloaded the photos and **restarted** when it was empty.*

3 Complete the sentences using the verbs in the box.

enable	lock	install	charge

1 If you .... a feature, then you make it work / function.

2 If you .... a piece of equipment, then you set it so that it will not turn on.

3 If you .... a battery, then you give it energy so that it works.

4 If you .... a piece of equipment, then you make it ready to use.

4 Read the problems and choose the best advice.

1 I can't switch my camera on. The batteries are charged and installed correctly. What could be the problem?

   a The camera might be locked. Remove the batteries and memory card and wait for at least five minutes before trying again.

   b The batteries might be too cold. Take them out and warm them in your pocket before trying again.

2 Where can I find more information about installing the batteries?

   a page 18

   b page 8

3 What should I do if my memory card is full?

   a Set the camera to playback mode.

   b Download the photographs to your computer and delete them from the memory card.

4 My viewfinder is blank – I've checked the power-saving isn't enabled. What should I try now?

   a Reset the camera by removing the batteries and memory card and waiting five minutes before putting them back and trying again.

   b The batteries might be too cold. Take them out and warm them in your pocket before trying again.

My review

I can read and follow step by step instructions.	☐
I can troubleshoot a problem by checking the instructions.	☐
I can understand the labels on a picture.	☐

APPENDIX 1 – How should I read?

Every day you read all sorts of different things, from signs in the streets to newspapers, labels on medicine bottles and your favourite websites. Do you read all these things in the same way?

Learning how to read in English is just as important as understanding grammar and vocabulary. Over the next two pages, we look at different ways of reading quickly and reading carefully, so that you can improve each method. Note, however, that all these methods are linked. For example, you may read through a text quickly to find out the main idea before reading it carefully for general understanding; or you may read a text quickly to find a specific section before reading that section carefully for detail.

Reading quickly

In some situations, you have to be able to read quickly. There are two ways to do this.

Reading quickly to get the general idea (skimming)

You read in this way when you have a limited amount of time, but want a general idea of what the text is about.

Use skimming for:

- a quick read of a newspaper or magazine article.
- a first read-through of a website to see if it's of interest to you.
- a first read-through of a sign or notice to see if it's relevant to you.

Improving your skimming skills

- Choose a text (for example, a newspaper article) and set yourself a short time limit (for example, two minutes). Read through quickly all the way to the end. Then write a summary sentence about the main point of the article. Reread the article more carefully and compare it with your summary sentence.
- Keep your eyes moving forwards. Use a marker to cover up the line you have just read to stop yourself from looking back.
- Do not look up any unknown vocabulary. Try to read it all the way to the end and then look back and see if you really need to look up words to understand the main idea of the text.
- If you are very short on time, read just the title, first and last paragraphs and the topic sentences (first sentence of each paragraph), which will often be enough to give you the main idea of an article.

Reading quickly to find specific information (scanning)

You read in this way when you have a limited amount of time, and you want to find out something specific from a text.

Use scanning for:

- a timetable to see what time your train is leaving.
- the television listings to see what's on now.
- looking for a word in a dictionary.
- looking for particular information or the correct link on a website.
- using the contents page or index to find a particular section of a book.
- looking in a newspaper to find an article that interests you.

Improving your scanning skills

- Do not read every word, but pass your eyes over the text looking just for the information you need. Some people scan paragraphs diagonally. Others read down the page in the shape of a 'Z'. Find the method that works best for you.
- Practise looking for particular pieces of information in a text – for example, if you are looking for numbers, make your eyes stop at digits; if you are looking for titles, stop when you see capital letters or italics.
- Don't be distracted by information that you don't need. Ignore these sections of text.
- When you find the piece of information that you need, you may then have to read that section carefully.

Reading carefully

In some situations, you need to read a text carefully. There are two ways to do this.

Reading carefully for general understanding

You read in this way when you have plenty of time and you want a good understanding of what the text is about.

Use this method for reading:

- a newspaper or magazine story that interests you.
- a blog or website that interests you.
- an email from a friend.

Improving this reading method

- Choose reading materials that interest you … this sort of reading should be fun!
- Read as much as you can and whenever you can. The more you read, the easier it becomes.
- To improve your reading speed, run a finger or pen beneath each line of a book as you read, keeping it moving steadily and not stopping to look up unknown words. Then go back over the text at the end and use a dictionary to help you with any key vocabulary.

Reading carefully to understand every detail

You read in this way when you have plenty of time and you need to understand every single detail of the text.

Use this method for reading:

- instructions for equipment.
- signs that contain important information relevant to you.
- labels on medicine bottles.

Improving this reading method

- Use your dictionary as often as you need to – when reading for detail, you often need to understand every word.
- Sometimes instruction booklets will include instructions in many different languages. Start by reading the English and work out exactly what you need to do, looking up as many words as necessary. Then check against the instructions in your own language to see if you have understood every detail correctly.

APPENDIX 2 – Practical reading study tips

While you read

Using a dictionary

A dictionary is very important, but don't become too dependent on it. When reading a text for the first time, try not to open your dictionary at all. When you finish, summarize the main points (*see Writing a summary* below). Then go back and reread the text more carefully, looking up unknown words. Then look again at your summary to see whether you really needed to use your dictionary to understand the main points of the text. See page 102 for more tips on using a dictionary.

Keeping a vocabulary notebook

When you have finished reading a text, go back over it and write down any useful new words in a vocabulary notebook. Organize this topic-by-topic or letter-by-letter and try to learn several new words every day. Test yourself by rereading texts that you have read before to see if you can remember the words that you wrote down in your notebook the first time.

Using a pen/pencil

You might find it useful to read texts with a pen or pencil in hand.

- Underline important sentences or phrases while you are reading.
- Write notes to summarize paragraphs.
- Try using different highlighter pens to colour-code new vocabulary.

Taking notes

A good way to check that you understand what you are reading is to take notes on a text:

- As you read a text or section of text, underline or highlight key sentences or words.
- When you have finished, look back over the highlighted sentences or words and pull out the main ideas – you can leave out details, examples and illustrations.
- Don't copy sections of text – write notes using your own words.
- Don't write full sentences, just the important words.
- Use shortened forms that you understand.
- Finally, reread the text and compare it to your notes to make sure that you have included all the main points.

Writing a summary

To summarize a text, you must pull out the main points of a text and write them in a shorter form (usually between 15 and 20% of the original).

- First, take notes on the main ideas of the text (see *Taking notes above*).
- Then, turn the notes into full sentences.
- Finally, compare the text with your summary to ensure that you have included all the main points.

Within the text

Contents list

A contents list is a good place to start when trying to find a particular section of a book. You do not have to read every word in the contents – ignore words at the beginning such as 'introduction' or 'how to use this book' and at the end such as 'appendix', 'glossary', or 'index'. Instead, focus on the chapter headings to give you an idea of how the book is divided up and look for key words about the section you are looking for.

Topic sentences

The first sentence of each paragraph (the topic sentence) often summarizes what the whole paragraph is about. This is helpful when you are reading quickly to find the main idea of a text because you can work out what it is about by simply reading the topic sentences.

Signposting language

Watch out for words and phrases that a writer uses to help you find your way around the text. For example, they may order a list of items with 'firstly,' 'secondly,' 'thirdly,' and 'finally'. See page 100 for more examples of this.

Illustrations and pictures

Illustrations such as graphs or maps are useful in helping you to understand the text. If you are just reading quickly to find the main idea, make sure you also look at any pictures and their captions that might help you to understand the text.

Using the Internet

Search engines

- Write as many key words as you can in a search engine to make the results as useful as possible.
- When you click on one of the search results, look at the webpage quickly checking for key words to see if the page is useful.
- If it is useful then take the time to read it carefully, but if it isn't, then move on to the next webpage in the search results.

Search by reading level

Google has a very helpful search tool, which sorts webpages by reading level. To do this, search for your topic as usual, then on the left hand side of the screen, click on, 'More search tools,' and from this menu, click on, 'Reading level'. Then click on your reading level ('Basic,' 'Intermediate' or 'Advanced') and it will list just these pages for you.

Learn how to read more quickly

Choose the right thing to read

People usually read more quickly when they enjoy what they are reading, so make sure that:
- you're interested in what you're reading. Try reading a wide variety of different texts to find things you like. If you're interested in the story, then you're more likely to read (quickly) to the end.

- the text is at the right language level for you. If it's too easy, you will get bored and if it's too difficult, you will get lost.

Skim read first

Skim read first to work out the main idea of a text. Then when you read the text in detail, you will understand it more quickly.

This does not work for longer texts, for example novels, but can be used with shorter texts, for example websites or newspaper articles.

Read chunks of text

Reading a text is like doing a jigsaw – you must put together the individual words to understand the whole. A jigsaw with lots of small pieces takes much longer than one with just a few large pieces. So, try reading chunks of text (three to five words) instead of reading each word individually. For example, when reading this sentence from Unit 18, you can group together the following chunks:

'I ask him if / it feels as though / he is living / in a golden prison / from which he escapes / only to play football.'

You can group words:

- linked by meaning, for example: 'play football';
- or linked by language function – for example, group articles and adjectives with their nouns ('a golden prison') or verbs with their person ('he is living').

Use a pointer

Try moving your finger or a pen under each line of a book as you read and do not stop to look up unknown words. Don't go back and reread sentences because this will slow you down. If you find this difficult, use a piece of paper or a ruler to cover up the line you have just read to stop you going back. Look up any new words that you still think are important at the end.

Read in your head

Don't read aloud and don't even move your lips silently when you're reading quickly because this will stop you from reading any faster than you can speak, even though your brain can take in information much more quickly than this. However, reading aloud is useful when you want to practise your pronunciation.

Focus on important words

When reading, some words are more important than others. Focus on the words that carry the meaning, for example, the nouns, verbs, and adjectives; pay less attention to the words that hold the sentence together, for example, conjunctions, prepositions, or articles. In the sentence below, you can focus on the words in bold and let your eyes skim over the other words:

*E-readers have some **advantages**. They are **light** and **hard-wearing** and can **last weeks** on a **single charge**.*

APPENDIX 3 – Reading specific text types

Some text types have their own unique vocabulary and some are suited to particular styles of reading. Here are some tips to help you to read and understand specific types of text.

Reading texts with specific vocabulary

Reading text-speak

Texting has created a completely new form of English, which is still taking shape and so is not always consistent. The aim of text-speak is to limit the number of keys you have to press:

- Letters are used to replace whole words (e.g., 'c' instead of 'see', 'u' instead of 'you').
- Numbers are used instead of letters where possible (e.g. ,'2' instead of 'to', 'gr8' instead of 'great').
- Vowels are often dropped (e.g., 'n' instead of 'and') or shortened (e.g., 'gud' instead of 'good').
- Acronyms (words formed from the first letters of a phrase) are widely used (e.g., 'lol' instead of 'laugh out loud' or 'IMO' instead of 'in my opinion').
- Emoticons or smileys are used to show how the person is feeling (e.g., '☺' instead of 'I'm happy').

Understanding Twitter terminology

There are some language features that are unique to Twitter:

DMKimKid DJ

@Beatbopno1fan

These are two ways of sending somebody a personal message on Twitter. 'DM' is a direct message and will be seen only by the named follower. '@' replies will appear in the person's timeline and can be seen by other users too.

 **Retweet**

This link means 'Retweet' where you repost (or repeat) something that has already been said by another Twitter user.

Worldwide Trends
#Leah Potts

Topics that are being discussed by lots of users are said to be 'trending' and a list of current trending topics is visible on your homepage. Users tag their Tweets with a hashtag (#) to link it to the debate.

See 'Twitter conventions' on page 96 for some short forms that are used on Twitter.

Reading shortened forms on social networking sites

The language used on social networking sites is closer to spoken English than written English. You often see shortened versions of words (for example, 'thx' instead of 'thanks') and grammatical forms (for example, 'Having a great day' instead of 'I'm having a great day'). Appendix 4 provides some examples of shortened forms that you will commonly see on social networking sites.

Reading texts in a specific way

Reading signs and notices

First, read signs and notices quickly to find out if they are relevant to you. If they are, then read them again very carefully for detail making sure that you understand every word. Sometimes the information that they contain is very important, for example fire notices, airport security notices or train departure times.

Reading step-by-step instructions

Always start by reading the instructions quickly all the way to the end to get a rough idea of what you have to do. Then read each step carefully. Make sure that you understand exactly what the instructions are telling you to do before you start to follow them – this will help you to avoid making mistakes. Also, look closely at the pictures because they can help you understand difficult words.

Reading newspaper and magazine stories

Newspaper and magazine stories are often organized in this way:

- The headline is a short summary of the story (not always a full sentence) that is designed to grab your attention and make you want to read the whole story.
- The first paragraph is a summary of the story.
- The rest of the text looks at the story in depth, answering the questions: What? When? Where? Who? Why?

You need to use a number of reading styles for newspapers. First, pass your eyes quickly over the headlines until you find a story that interests you. Then read the first paragraph quickly for a summary of the story. If you want to know more about the story, then read the rest of it carefully for general understanding.

Reading directions

Always read directions carefully before you begin your journey to make sure that you understand exactly what they are telling you to do. Look also at any maps that you are given and use them to help you to understand the text.

Reading medicine bottles and labels

Always read this information very carefully for detail and make sure that you understand every word. It is very important to find out if the medicine is safe to take along with any others you might be taking and also to be clear about how much you should take and how often.

Reading reviews and blogs

Don't believe everything you read! When reading a review or a blog, remember that this is only one person's opinion and so is not necessarily true.

APPENDIX 4 – Understanding short forms of English

When you are reading, you may see short forms of English. These lists will help you to understand what they mean.

Emoticons in texts and instant messages

:)	smiling / happy
:(	sad / unhappy
;)	joking / don't take this seriously
:D	big grin / happy
<3	heart / love
</3	broken heart / no love
\o/	excitement / jumping for joy
:0	surprise / shocked face
d(^_^)b	headphones / listening to music
(^_-)	winking
o∧o	high five
:-P	sticking your tongue out at someone (cheeky, not rude)
:X	'my lips are sealed' (= I'm not telling you anything)
@}-;--	rose / romantic

Symbols

&	and
+	plus
=	equals / is the same as
≠	does not equal / is not the same as
>	is greater than
<	is less than
"	repeat the text that you see above
@	at
→	connects two ideas
←	connects two ideas
?	don't know / not sure
↑	increasing
↓	decreasing
∴	therefore
#	number
$	dollars / money

Short forms of words

Use these in emails or instant messages to people you know well, as well as to take notes.

abt.   about

b/c	because
c.	circa (around the time)
cf.	compare
ch.	chapter
D.O.B.	date of birth
e.g.	for example
esp.	especially
etc.	and all the rest
govt.	government
i.e.	that is / in other words
max.	maximum
min.	minimum
mth.	month
no. / nos.	number / numbers
N.B.	important
p. / pp.	page / pages
re.	concerning / about
sbd.	somebody
sth.	something
vs.	versus (meaning 'against')
w/	with
w/o	without
yr.	year

You will probably see a number of different ways of writing short forms. A good rule to remember is 'use a full stop if the final letter is missing, but don't if it's present'. So:

st abt yr vs govt   but   c. sbd. max. etc.

Understanding Twitter conventions

RT	= Retweet	A Retweet is when a person reposts (or repeats) something that has already been Tweeted by another person.
	= modified (changed) Tweet	Use when you have shortened someone else's Tweet so you can Retweet it. Make sure you don't change the meaning of the original Tweet when you shorten it.
DM	= direct (private) message	A direct message (followed by a person's name) is a way of sending a private Tweet to somebody.
@	= at replies	An @ message (followed by a person's name) is a way of sending a personal Tweet to somebody. These messages are not private and can be seen by anyone.
#	= hashtag	Hashtags are used to link Tweets to particular subjects that other users are also Tweeting about. Hashtagged subjects are often trending (being Tweeted about by lots of users) and a list of trending subjects appear on your homepage.
	= square brackets	Use these when you want to add a comment of your own after another Tweet. E.g. RT @madonnafanclubLondon Great concert last night! [Yes! It was wonderful!]
#FF	= follow Friday	Follow Fridays are used on Fridays to recommend new people to follow.

APPENDIX 5 – Understanding punctuation

Exclamation marks (!) and question marks (?)

Exclamation marks are used:

- in exclamations, for example:
  Wow!, Yes!, Hi!
- to show surprise, for example:
  Leah Potts is trending worldwide!
- to show excitement, for example:
  You can LIVE English rather than LEARN or STUDY it!
- to add emphasis, for example:
  Real English fiction – that's real English language!

Question marks are used:

- at the end of direct questions:
  Where are you from?

In informal written English, we can use more than one exclamation mark or question mark or even both together to add emphasis, for example:

I really like the Beatbops!!!

You did what???

Someone explain to me why Leah Potts is trending??!!

Apostrophes

Apostrophes are used:

- to show that a letter has been removed, for example:
  That's [instead of that is] *what I'm* [instead of I am] *trying to do.*
- to show singular possession, we use 's, for example:
  the boy's e-book [the e-book belongs to one boy]
- to show plural possession, we use s', for example:
  the boys' e-book [the e-book belongs to more than one boy]

Bullet points

Bullet points are used in lists, for example:

Three types of appointments are available:

- *appointments made in advance.*
- *same-day appointments.*
- *emergency appointments.*

Recognizing forms of punctuation (the symbols used in writing) can help you to understand a text when you are reading it.

Punctuation in dialogue

When reading dialogue in a text, remember that the words of each speaker are set in quotation marks, either single ('for example') or double ("for example").

The words of each new speaker start on a new line. This will help you to keep track of who is saying what:

'So are you the classic pibe?' I ask Messi.

'That's what I'm trying to do,' he says. 'Football is a game. I'm trying to have fun. The day I stop having fun is the day I retire.'

Round and square brackets

Round brackets can be used to explain or clarify, for example:

Place any pocket items (for example, mobile, coins, keys, etc.) in a basket.

They can also be used to make an additional comment, for example:

Coffee (free refills!) $1.95

Square brackets are used to insert some form of explanation that was not included in the original version of a text, for example:

I would love to go [home] with the e-reader during the holidays.

Dashes

Dashes can be used in the same way as brackets to make an additional comment, for example:

Remove the batteries and memory card and wait – for at least five minutes – before reinserting them.

A dash can also be used to add an afterthought to the end of a sentence, for example:

Early results are good, says Mr Risher – in Worldreader's first test, they found that primary-school students who got e-readers improved their reading on tests from about 13% to 16%.

Dashes can also be used to show a range of values, for example:

Mon–Sat, 10am–6pm

APPENDIX 6 – Signposting language

When reading, look out for signposting language that is used by the writer to help you to find your way around the text.

To order a list of items

to begin with	next
first(ly)	after
second(ly)	in the end
third(ly)	finally
then	lastly

To present the most important point

above all	especially
most importantly	in particular

To make an additional point

and	what is more
too	in addition
also	above all
furthermore	then
again	as well as

To present an example

for example	as
e.g.	such as
for instance	including
say	

To show results or consequence

so	for this/that reason
therefore	because
as a result	as
in this way	for
then	

To show contrast or balance

but	yet
however	anyway
or	even so
in contrast	although
in comparison	otherwise
on the other hand	still
then	besides
instead	

To restate an argument or point

in other words	to put it simply

To make a point strongly

of course	clearly
naturally	certainly
obviously	

To finish

in conclusion	to summarize
to conclude	overall
to sum up	then
in brief	

APPENDIX 7 – Using a dictionary

A dictionary is very important when you are reading English. It is also important to learn when and how to use your dictionary in the best way.

When to use a dictionary

When you're reading, don't look up every new word. Instead, try to look up only the words that hold the meaning of the text. You can practise this. Read a paragraph from start to finish without looking in your dictionary. Then check if you have understood the main idea of it. If you do understand, then you don't need to use your dictionary here. If you don't understand, go back over the paragraph and look up the most important words until you get the main idea of the text.

How to use the mini-dictionary in this book

Dictionary entries are ordered alphabetically from A–Z. Every entry starts with a **headword** set in bold like this.

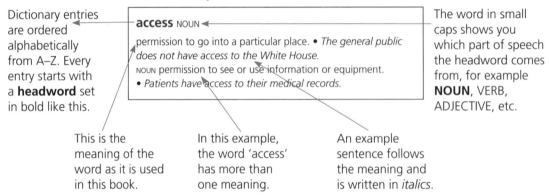

access NOUN

permission to go into a particular place. • *The general public does not have access to the White House.*

NOUN permission to see or use information or equipment. • *Patients have access to their medical records.*

The word in small caps shows you which part of speech the headword comes from, for example **NOUN**, VERB, ADJECTIVE, etc.

This is the meaning of the word as it is used in this book.

In this example, the word 'access' has more than one meaning.

An example sentence follows the meaning and is written in *italics*.

How to use a full dictionary

Different dictionaries can be quite different in style but these are some of the most common things you might see:

- **Running heads:** You will usually see running heads at the top of each page to help you to find your way around the dictionary. On left-hand pages, the running head is the same as the first complete entry on that page. On right-hand pages, it's the same as the last entry that begins on that page.

- **Usage labels:** You may see usage labels for some words, for example 'formal' or 'informal' to help you understand when particular words are used.

- **Pronunciation:** You may see the word set in the International Phonetic Alphabet to help you to understand its pronunciation, for example 'access' would be spelt /'ækses/. If these symbols are used, you will find the key to them at the front or back of the dictionary.

When you have finished using the dictionary, write useful new words in your own vocabulary notebook to help you to remember them.

MINI-DICTIONARY

 Some of the more difficult words from each unit are defined here in this Mini-dictionary. The definitions focus on the meanings of the words in the contexts in which they appear in the book. The examples are from the Collins COBUILD Corpus.

Unit 1

architect NOUN
a person whose job is to design buildings

carnival NOUN
a party in the street, with music and dancing • *The carnival went on all night long.*

chat NOUN
an informal and friendly conversation • *I had a chat with John.*

chatroom NOUN
a website where people can exchange messages • *A chatroom is a great place to make new friends.*

forum NOUN
a place on the Internet where people can have discussions • *The website has a forum where problems can be discussed.*

greet VERB
to say 'Hello' to someone • *She greeted him when he came home from school.*

improve VERB
to get better • *Their French improved during their trip to Paris.*

interesting ADJECTIVE
making you want to know more about something • *London is a very interesting city.*

meet VERB
to see someone who you do not know and speak to them for the first time • *I have just met an amazing man.*

nationality NOUN
the state of being a legal citizen of a particular country • *I'm not sure of her nationality, but I think she's Canadian.*

practise VERB
to do something often in order to do it better • *Keep practising, and next time you'll do better.*

socialise VERB
to meet other people socially, for example at parties • *I like socialising and making new friends.*

waiter NOUN
a man whose job is to serve food in a restaurant

webpage or **web page** NOUN
a set of information that you can see on a computer screen as part of a website

website or **web site** NOUN
a set of information about a particular subject that is available on the Internet

Unit 2

comment VERB
to give your opinion or say something about something • *Mr Cooke has not commented on these reports.*

congratulate VERB
to express pleasure about something good that has happened to someone • *She congratulated him on the birth of his son.*

homepage NOUN
the main page of a person's or an organization's website • *The company offers a number of services on its homepage.*

like VERB
to think a thing is interesting, enjoyable or attractive • *He likes baseball.*

marathon NOUN
a race in which people run a distance of 26 miles (= about 42 km) • *He is running in his first marathon next weekend.*

particular ADJECTIVE
used for showing that you are talking about one thing or one type of thing rather than other similar ones • *I have to know exactly why I'm doing a particular job.*

personal information NOUN
details about a person and their life, such as their age or where they live • *How much personal information should you put on a website?*

post VERB
to put information on a website so that other people can see it • *The statement was posted on the Internet.*

social networking site NOUN
a website on which you can contact friends, share information and make new friends • *Have you used a social networking site such as MySpace or Facebook?*

stay in touch VERB
to write or speak to someone regularly • *My brother and I stay in touch by phone.*

terrible ADJECTIVE
causing great pain or sadness • *Thousands of people suffered terrible injuries.*

Unit 3

abbreviation NOUN
a short form of a word or phrase • *The abbreviation for 'page' is 'p.'*

angry ADJECTIVE
feeling a strong emotion when someone has done something bad, or someone has treated you unfairly • *We are angry about the decision to close the school.*

be interested in doing something VERB
to want to spend time doing something • *I'm interested in finding out more about space.*

booked up ADJECTIVE
with no places left for a particular time or date • *The hotel is booked up until August.*

confused ADJECTIVE
not understanding what is happening, or not knowing what to do • *People are confused about what's going to happen.*

delivery NOUN
the goods that are delivered • *I got a delivery of fresh eggs this morning.*

excited ADJECTIVE
very happy or enthusiastic • *I was excited about playing football again.*

Unit 4

adore VERB
to like something very much • *Richard adores university life.*

amazing ADJECTIVE
very surprising, in a way that you like • *It's amazing what we can remember if we try.*

artificial ADJECTIVE
something that does not occur naturally • *The plants in my office are artificial.*

awful ADJECTIVE
very bad • *I thought he was an awful actor.*

celebrity NOUN
someone who is famous • *Madonna is a celebrity.*

cool ADJECTIVE
fashionable and interesting • *She had really cool boots.*

contain VERB
to have other things inside • *The envelope contained a Christmas card.*

discover VERB
to become aware of something that you did not know about before • *After a short conversation, she discovered the reason for his unhappiness.*

fact NOUN
something that you know is true • *He doesn't hide the fact that he wants to win.*

fiction NOUN
books and stories about people and events that are not real • *Many authors prefer to write fiction.*

great ADJECTIVE
very good • *I thought it was a great idea.*

love VERB to like something or someone very much • *I love food, I love cooking and I love eating.*

opinion NOUN
what someone thinks about something • *I didn't ask for your opinion.*

Unit 5

accommodation NOUN
buildings or rooms where people live or stay • *Many universities provide student accommodation.*

advanced ADJECTIVE
relating to people who are very good at something • *a dictionary for advanced learners of English*

amazing ADJECTIVE
very surprising, in a way that you like • *It's amazing what we can remember if we try.*

beginner NOUN
someone who has just started to do or learn something • *The course is for both beginners and advanced students.*

date of birth NOUN
the day, month and year that you were born • *Please write your name, address and date of birth.*

elementary ADJECTIVE
very easy and basic • *It's a simple system that uses elementary mathematics.*

extra-curricular activities PLURAL NOUN
activities that take place outside the normal school timetable • *The school organises extra-curricular activities such as sport and drama.*

FAQ NOUN (or FAQs PLURAL NOUN)
often written on websites to mean 'frequently asked questions'

intermediate ADJECTIVE
in the middle level, between two other levels • *We teach beginner, intermediate and advanced level students.*

luxury NOUN
something pleasant and expensive that people want but do not really need • *Having a holiday is a luxury they can no longer afford.*

registration form NOUN
a list of questions with spaces where you should put the answers, which you use to put your name on a list, in order to be able to do a particular thing • *To apply for the course, complete the online registration form.*

surname NOUN
the name that you share with other members of your family • *'And what's your surname, please?'—'Mitchell.'*

terms PLURAL NOUN
the conditions that all of the people involved in an arrangement must agree to • *The terms of the agreement are quite simple.*

Unit 6

access NOUN
permission to go into a particular place • *The general public does not have access to the White House.* NOUN permission to see or use information or equipment • *Patients have access to their medical records.*

available ADJECTIVE
that you can use or get • *Breakfast is available from 6 a.m.*

belongings PLURAL NOUN
the things that you own • *I gathered my belongings and left.*

cloud NOUN
a white or grey thing in the sky that is made of drops of water • *Clouds began to form in the sky*

conference NOUN
a long meeting about a particular subject • *We attended a conference on education last month.*

discover VERB
to find something • *The car was discovered on a roadside outside the city.*

facilities PLURAL NOUN
something such as rooms, buildings or pieces of equipment that are used for a particular purpose • *The hotel has excellent sports facilities, including a golf course.*

fully-equipped ADJECTIVE
having all the pieces of equipment that are needed for a particular purpose • *Each apartment has a fully-equipped kitchen with a cooker and refrigerator.*

operate VERB
to make a machine work • *Robert showed him how to operate the machine.*

proceed VERB
to go in a particular direction • *He proceeded down the street.*

rain NOUN
water that falls from the clouds in small drops • *We got very wet in the rain.*

rainy ADJECTIVE
raining a lot • *Here are some fun things to do on a rainy day.*

reception NOUN
the desk in a hotel or a large building that you go to when you first arrive • *She was waiting at reception.*

safe NOUN
a strong metal box with a lock, where you keep money or other valuable things • *Who has the key to the safe?*

sauna NOUN
a very hot room that is filled with steam, where people relax • *The hotel has a sauna and a swimming pool.*

sunny ADJECTIVE
with the sun shining brightly • *The weather was warm and sunny.*

suspect VERB
to think that something is true although you are not certain about it • *He suspected that she was telling lies.*

wheelchair NOUN
a chair with wheels that you use if you cannot walk very well • *My grandfather sometimes uses a wheelchair.*

wind NOUN
air that moves • *A strong wind was blowing from the north.*

windy ADJECTIVE
with a lot of wind • *It was a wet and windy day.*

Unit 7

acre NOUN
a unit for measuring an area of land • *William farms a hundred acres of land in Wales.*

admission NOUN
the amount of money that you pay to enter a museum, park or other place • *Gates open at 10.30 a.m. and admission is free.* NOUN permission to enter a place • *This ticket for the museum includes admission to the museum gardens.*

adult NOUN
a fully grown person • *Tickets cost $20 for adults and $10 for children.*

atmosphere NOUN
the general feeling that you get when you are in a place • *The rooms are warm and the atmosphere is welcoming.*

concessions PLURAL NOUN
special prices which are lower than the usual prices and which are often given to old people, students, and the unemployed • *Admission £5 with concessions for children and students.*

discount NOUN
a reduction in the usual price of something • *All staff get a 20% discount.*

ID NOUN
a document that shows who you are • *I had no ID so I couldn't prove that it was my car.*

landmark NOUN
a well-known building or other object in a particular place • *The Empire State Building is a New York landmark.*

performance NOUN
when you entertain an audience by singing, dancing or acting • *They were giving a performance of Bizet's `Carmen'.*

sightseeing NOUN
the activity of travelling around visiting the interesting places that tourists usually visit • *During our holiday, we had a day's sightseeing in Venice.*

tour NOUN
a trip to an interesting place or around several interesting places • *Michael took me on a tour of the nearby islands.*

view NOUN
everything that you can see from a place • *From our hotel room we had a great view of the sea.*

Unit 8

allow VERB
if you are allowed to do or have something, you have permission to do or have it • *I'm not allowed to go to the party.*

bakery NOUN
a place where bread and cakes are baked or sold • *The town has two bakeries.*

butcher NOUN
a shop where you can buy meat

cashier NOUN
who customers pay money to or get money from in places such as shops or banks • *John is waiting in the queue to pay the cashier.*

change NOUN
the money that you get back when you pay with more money than something costs • *`There's your change.'—`Thanks very much.'*

chemist NOUN
a shop that sells medicines, make-up and some other things

department store NOUN
a large shop that sells many different types of goods

exchange NOUN
the act of taking something back to a shop and getting a different thing • *If you are unhappy with the product, return it for an exchange.*

gift NOUN
something that you give to someone as a present • *We gave her a birthday gift.*

price NOUN
the amount of money that you have to pay in order to buy something • *They expect house prices to rise.*

purchase NOUN
the act of buying something • *The Canadian company announced the purchase of 1,663 shops in the U.S.*

receipt NOUN
a piece of paper that shows that you have received goods or money from someone • *I gave her a receipt for the money.*

reduction NOUN
when something is made smaller or less • *We have noticed a sudden reduction in prices.*

refund NOUN
money that is returned to you because you have paid too much, or because you have returned goods to a

shop • *He took the boots back to the shop and asked for a refund.*

return VERB
to give back or put back something that you borrowed or took • *They will return the money later.* NOUN something you take back to a shop because you don't want to keep it • *Please contact the manager for all returns.*

sale NOUN
a time when a shop sells things at less than their normal price • *Did you know the bookshop was having a sale?*

stock NOUN
the total amount of goods that a shop has available to sell • *Most of the stock was destroyed in the fire.*

supermarket NOUN
a large shope that sells all kinds of food and other products for the home • *We mostly do our food shopping in the supermarket.*

till NOUN
a machine that holds money in a shop • *She took some money from the till.*

Unit 9

appetizer NOUN
a small amount of food that you eat as the first part of a meal • *There was a choice of three appetizers and three mains on the menu.*

boil VERB
to cook food in boiling water • *Wash and boil the rice.*

delicious ADJECTIVE
very good to eat • *There was a wide choice of delicious meals.*

dessert NOUN
something sweet that you eat at the end of a meal • *We had ice cream for dessert.*

disappointing ADJECTIVE
not as good as you hoped it would be • *The movie I saw last night was disappointing.*

disgusting ADJECTIVE
extremely unpleasant or unacceptable • *The food tasted disgusting.*

excellent ADJECTIVE
extremely good • *The quality of these photographs is excellent.*

fry VERB
to cook food in hot fat or oil • *Fry the onions until they are brown.*

grill VERB
to cook food on metal bars above a fire or barbecue or under a grill • *grilled fish*

main NOUN
the biggest and most important dish of a meal • *Dessert is served after the main.*

refill NOUN
another drink to replace one already drunk • *Max asked for a refill and held out his cup.*

side NOUN
a dish that is served to accompany the main meal • *I had salad as a side.*

terrible ADJECTIVE
extremely bad • *I have a terrible singing voice.*

yummy ADJECTIVE
having a pleasant flavour and being good to eat • *The food here is yummy.*

Unit 10

booking fee NOUN
an extra amount of money that is sometimes added on when you buy tickets • *Tickets for the event will cost £20 plus booking fee.*

cast NOUN
all the people who act in a play or a film • *The show is very amusing and the case is very good.*

confirm VERB
to say that a meeting or an arrangement will definitely happen • *He called at seven to confirm our appointment.*

origins PLURAL NOUN
the way something started • *Scientists study the origins of life on Earth.*

passion NOUN
a very strong feeling about something or a strong belief in something • *He spoke with great passion.*

politics PLURAL NOUN
the activities and ideas that are concerned with government • *He was involved in local politics.*

purchase NOUN
the act of buying something • *The Canadian company announced the purchase of 1,663 shops in the U.S.*

quantity NOUN
an amount • *Pour a small quantity of water into a pan.*

reserved ADJECTIVE
when something is kept specially for that person • *This table is reserved for us.*

science fiction NOUN
stories in books, magazines and films about things that happen in the future or in other parts of the universe

superb ADJECTIVE
very good • *There is a superb golf course 6 miles away.*

terrific ADJECTIVE
very good • *What a terrific idea!*

total NOUN
the number that you get when you add several numbers together • *Add all the amounts together, and subtract ten from the total.*

Unit 11

allergic ADJECTIVE
becoming ill when you eat, touch or breathe something that does not usually affect people in this way • *I'm allergic to cats.*

appointment NOUN
an arrangement to see someone at a particular time • *She has an appointment with her doctor.*

dosage NOUN
the amount that should be taken of a medicine or drug • *The dosage for the cough medicine is written on the box.*

effective ADJECTIVE
producing the results that you want • *No drugs are effective against this disease.*

emergency NOUN
a serious situation, such as an accident, when people need help quickly • *Come quickly. This is an emergency!*

liquid NOUN
a substance that is not a solid or a gas. Liquids flow and can be poured. Water and oil are liquids. • *She took out a small bottle of clear liquid.*

overdose VERB
to take more of a medicine than is safe • *She overdosed on paracetamol.* NOUN when you take more of a medicine than is recommended • *He died of an overdose.*

patient NOUN
a person who receives medical treatment from a doctor • *The patient was suffering from heart problems.*

pharmacy NOUN
a place where you can buy medicines • *Pick up the medicine from the pharmacy.*

pharmacist NOUN
a person whose job is to prepare and sell medicines • *Ask your pharmacist for advice.*

relief NOUN
when pain or worry stops • *These drugs will give relief from pain.*

side effects PLURAL NOUN
the effects a medicine has on you in addition to its function of curing illness or pain • *This medicine has unpleasant side-effects, such as nausea, vomiting and sweating.*

surgery NOUN
the room or house where a doctor or dentist works • *My doctor's surgery is on that street.* NOUN the period of time each day when a doctors sees patients • *Bring him along to the morning surgery.*

symptom NOUN
something that is wrong with you that is a sign of a particular illness • *All these patients have flu symptoms.*

Unit 12

baggage or **luggage** NOUN
all the bags that you take with you when you travel • *He collected his baggage and left the airport.*

boarding pass NOUN
a card that a passenger must show when they are entering an aircraft or a boat • *Please present your boarding pass before boarding the plane.*

business class NOUN
the part of a plane that is more expensive to travel in than economy class • *Kevin is flying business class for the first time.*

charge NOUN
an amount of money that you have to pay for a service • *We can arrange this for a small charge.*

economy class NOUN
the part of a plane that is cheapest to travel in • *He prefers to fly economy class, because it's cheaper.*

luggage see **baggage**

passenger NOUN
a person who is travelling in a vehicle such as a bus, a boat or a plane, but who is not driving it • *Mr Smith was a passenger in the car when it crashed.*

prohibited ADJECTIVE
officially illegal • *Smoking is prohibited here.*

restriction ADJECTIVE
an official rule that limits the amount or size of something • *The airline has restrictions on what objects you can bring onto the plane.*

valuables PLURAL NOUN
things that you own that are worth a lot of money, especially small objects such as jewellery • *Susan keeps her valuables somewhere safe.*

weight NOUN
how heavy a person or thing is • *What is your weight?*

weigh VERB
to measure how heavy something or someone is • *Lisa weighed the boxes for postage.*

Unit 13

affect VERB
to cause someone or something to change in some way • *This area was badly affected by the earthquake.*

alarm NOUN
a piece of equipment that warns you of danger, for example, by making a noise • *The fire alarm woke us at 5 a.m.*

arrival NOUN
the time something comes from one place to somewhere else • *The train's arrival is at 5 p.m.*

between PREPOSITION
from one place to the other and back again • *I spend a lot of time travelling between Edinburgh and London.*

departure NOUN
the time something leaves from one place to go somewhere else • *The train's departure is at 10 p.m.*

divert VERB
to force something to use a different route • *The plane was diverted to Edinburgh Airport.*

duration NOUN
the length of time that an event lasts • *Courses are of two years' duration.*

extended VERB
to make something longer • *These treatments have extended the lives of people with cancer.*

fare NOUN
the money that you pay for a trip in a bus, a train, an aeroplane or a taxi • *The fare is £11 one way.*

option NOUN
a choice between two or more things • *We will consider all options before making a decision.*

out of order PHRASE
not working properly • *Their phone's out of order.*

schedule VERB
to arrange for something to happen at a particular time • *The meeting with Mr Bush is scheduled for tomorrow morning.*

unattended ADJECTIVE
not being watched or looked after • *An unattended bag was found at the airport.*

Unit 14

cancel VERB
to stop an order or arrangement from happening • *Many trains have been cancelled today.*

concession NOUN
a cheaper ticket for a particular group of people • *If you're a student you're entitled to concessions on public transport.*

delay VERB
to make someone or something late • *Passengers were delayed at the airport for five hours.*

due ADJECTIVE
expected to happen or arrive at a particular time • *The results are due at the end of the month.*

increase NOUN
the amount by which something is made bigger in some way • *There was a sudden increase in the cost of oil.*

off-peak fare NOUN
the price of a travel ticket when the service is not busy and the ticket is cheaper • *After 6 p.m. you can buy a ticket at an off-peak fare.*

on time PHRASE
not late or early • *The train arrived at the station on time at eleven thirty.*

peak-rate fare NOUN
the price of a travel ticket when the service is busy and the ticket is more expensive • *Between 7 a.m. and 8 a.m., you have to buy a ticket at a peak-rate fare.*

proof NOUN
something that shows that something else is true or exists • *The scientists hope to find proof that there is water on Mars.*

valid ADJECTIVE
used for saying that a ticket can be used and will be accepted • *All tickets are valid for two months.*

Unit 15

access NOUN
permission to go into a particular place • *The general public does not have access to the White House.* NOUN permission to see or use information or equipment • *Patients have access to their medical records.*

arrow NOUN
a written sign that points in a particular direction • *The arrow pointed down to the bottom of the page.*

destination NOUN
the place you are going to • *He wanted to arrive at his destination before dark.*

detour NOUN
a route on a journey which is not the shortest way that you might take to avoid something such as a traffic jam • *He took a detour on his way to work.*

directions PLURAL NOUN
instructions that tell you what to do, how to do something, or how to get somewhere • *She stopped the car to ask for directions.*

distance NOUN
the amount of space between two places • *Measure the distance between the wall and the table.*

journey NOUN
an occasion when you travel from one place to another • *Their journey took them from Paris to Brussels.*

have priority PHRASE
to be more important than other things • *The needs of the schoolchildren always have priority.*

resident NOUN
a person who lives in a particular house or area • *My house has five residents.*

traffic NOUN
all the vehicles that are on a particular road at one time • *There was heavy traffic on the roads.* NOUN the movement of ships, trains or aircraft between one place and another • *No air traffic was allowed out of the airport.*

Unit 16

access NOUN
permission to go into a particular place • *The general public does not have access to the White House.*

accompanied by ADJECTIVE
joined by someone else when going somewhere • *Karen is accompanied by her two best friends.*

average NOUN
the result that you get when you add two or more amounts together and divide the total by the number of amounts you added together • *'What's the average of 4, 5 and 6?'–'5.'*

beware of PHRASE
to be careful because a person or a thing is dangerous • *Beware of the dangers of swimming in the sea at night.*

calories PLURAL NOUN
a unit that is used for measuring the amount of energy in food • *These sweet drinks have a lot of calories in them.*

current ADJECTIVE
happening now • *The current situation is different from the one in 1990.*

distance NOUN
the amount of space between two places • *Measure the distance between the wall and the table.*

hazard NOUN
something that could be dangerous • *Too much salt may be a health hazard.*

lane NOUN
a part of a road that is marked by a painted line • *The lorry was travelling at 20 mph in the slow lane.*

pedestrian NOUN
a person who is walking, especially in a town or city • *The city's pavements were busy with pedestrians.*

private ADJECTIVE
only for one particular person or group, and not for everyone • *It was a private conversation, so I'm not going to talk about it to anyone else.*

property NOUN
a building and the land around it (formal) • *Get out of here – this is private property!*

speed NOUN
how fast something moves or is done • *He drove off at high speed.*

Unit 17

advantage NOUN
a way in which one thing is better than another • *The advantage of home-grown vegetables is their great flavour.*

built-in ADJECTIVE
included in something else as an essential part of it • *There are built-in cupboards in the bedrooms.*

developing country NOUN
a poor country that does not have many industries • *Many students volunteer in developing countries, such as Haiti.*

digital ADJECTIVE
using information in the form of thousands of very small signals • *Most people now have digital television.*

e-reader NOUN
a device that you can carry with you and use to download and read texts in electronic form • *He read the entire Harry Potter series on his e-reader.*

hard-wearing ADJECTIVE
strong and well-made so that it lasts for a long time and stays in good condition even though it is used a lot • *I always wear hard-wearing shoes when I go mountain climbing.*

improve VERB
to get better • *Their French improved during their trip to Paris.*

non-profit organization NOUN
an organization which is not run with the aim of making a profit • *UNICEF is a famous non-profit organization.*

refugee NOUN
a person who has been forced to leave their home or their country, because it is too dangerous for them there • *She grew up in Britain as a refugee.*

revolution NOUN
an important change in a particular area of activity • *There was a revolution in ship design in the nineteenth century.*

Unit 18

achieve VERB
to succeed in doing something, usually after a lot of effort • *He worked hard to achieve his goals.*

attractively VERB
in a way that is pleasant • *His hair was attractively curly.*

brilliance VERB
exceptional talent • *Picasso is famous for his brilliance in painting.*

classic ADJECTIVE
of very good quality, and popular for a long time • *Fleming directed the classic film `The Wizard of Oz'.*

controlled ADJECTIVE
carefully thought about • *His behaviour is very controlled.*

determined ADJECTIVE
certain that you want to do something, no matter how difficult it is • *He is determined to win gold at the Olympics.*

grateful ADJECTIVE
wanting to thank someone for something that they give you or do for you • *She was grateful to him for being so helpful.*

hormone deficiency NOUN
the lack of a chemical substance in your body that affects the way your body works • *Children with growth hormone deficiency have problems growing.*

modest ADJECTIVE
not talking much about your abilities, skills or successes • *He's modest, as well as being a great player.*

retire VERB
to leave your job and usually stop working completely • *He planned to retire at 65.*

suffer from VERB
to be badly affected by a pain or illness • *She began to suffer from stomach cramps.*

Unit 19

for good PHRASE
used for saying that something has disappeared and will never come back • *These forests may be gone for good.*

in a flash PHRASE
when something happens very quickly • *The answer came to him in a flash.*

launch NOUN
the act of making a company's product available to the public • *The company's spending has risen following the launch of a new magazine.*

mark an anniversary VERB
to do something that shows you remember something special that happened on that date in an earlier year • *There will be special events to mark the anniversary of the battle.*

on the cards PHRASE
likely to happen • *An argument is on the cards.*

out of the question PHRASE
completely impossible • *An expensive holiday is out of the question for him.*

release VERB
to make a new CD, DVD or film available so that people can buy it or see it • *He is releasing a CD of love songs.*

sell out VERB
to not have any tickets left because they have all been sold • *Football games often sell out fast.*

split VERB
to separate and stop working as a group • *The band split after an argument.*

up for grabs PHRASE
when something is available to anyone who is interested
• *I've got a spare ticket to the football game, which is up for grabs.*

Unit 20

aim VERB
to point something toward a person or a thing • *He was aiming the gun at Wright.*

charged ADJECTIVE
containing enough electricity to to work • *A fully charged battery can last for two days.*

cover VERB
to put something over something else to protect it • *Cover the dish with a heavy lid.*

enabled ADJECTIVE
made to work • *Make sure the firewall on your computer is enabled.*

focus VERB
to make changes to a camera so that you can see clearly through it • *The camera was focused on his terrified face.*

locked ADJECTIVE
set so that it cannot be used without a special code • *If your phone is locked, it can't be used if it is stolen.*

press VERB
to push a button or a switch with your finger in order to make a machine work • *David pressed a button and the door closed.*

remove VERB
to take something away from a place • *Remove the cake from the oven when it is cooked.*

reset VERB
to set a device so that it is ready to work again • *I reset the alarm when I left the house.*

switch on VERB
to make an electronical device start working again by operating a switch • *We switched on the radio.*

view VERB
to look at • *Hundreds of people came to view the paintings.*

ANSWER KEY

Unit 1   Meeting and greeting

A   Meeting people online

1

b   where they come from and why they want to improve their English.

2

1   Hannah
2   Pedro
3   Li
4   Mariana

3

1   Hello! My name's Mariana and I'm from Brazil.
2   Hey! My name is Li and I'm Chinese.
3   Hello everyone! I'm Pedro, I'm Spanish and I live in Madrid.
4   Hi, I'm Hannah and I come from France.

B   Getting to know somebody online

1

2   True
3   False. Ava visted Visited Sao Paulo last year for the carnival.
4   False. Mariana does like the carnival.
5   False. Mariana is 23 years old.
6   False. Ava will be on EnglishClub tomorrow.

C   Finding new friends online

1

1   Name [✔]
2   Age [✔]
3   Nationality [✗]
4   Job [✔]
5   Languages they speak [✗]
6   Things they like to do in their free time [✔]

2

2   She's a sales assistant.
3   28
4   He wants to meet all sorts of different people.
5   Mariam
6   Robert

3

1   Mariam   3   Nicky
2   Robert   4   Paul

4

(Sample answer)

I would most like to meet Nicky because I like going to restaurants and shopping too.

5

Answers will vary. See Text C for model answer.

Unit 2   Staying in touch

A   Using social networking sites

1

1   d
2   e
3   b
4   c
5   a

2

	Have they posted on Friendsmeet?	If yes, what do they say?
Mary	Yes	She had a beautiful baby girl called Anna at 3am last night.
Yiannis	No	
Max	Yes	He thanks everyone for their birthday messages and says that he's having a great day.

3

2   True.

3   False. Mary had a baby daughter last night.

4   False. Daha Sharma broke his arm yesterday.

5   True

4

1   Congratulations!

2   Good luck!

3   That's terrible!

4   Oh, I don't!

5   Happy birthday!

B   Reading an email from a friend

1

Yiannis <u>finished</u> / didn't finish the marathon.

2

2   4 hours and 32 minutes

3   Very happy and very tired

4   How are you? / How are your English studies going?

5   His sister, her husband and their dog

6   Yiannis

3

(Sample answer)

Hi Yiannis,

Thanks for your email and congratulations on finishing the marathon!

I'm fine, thanks. My English is going well. I'm practising my reading a lot at the moment, which helps me to understand your emails!

Write soon.

Love,

Kim

Unit 3   Making plans

A   Reading texts to plan a social activity

1

1   f

2   c

3   a

4   e

5   d

6   b

2

2   Tomorrow morning at 10.30.

3   At Sophia's house

4   She has to be home for a delivery.

5   Her holiday photos / She is planning to go to Greece this year and wants to see what it's like.

3

2   Sorry I am/'m busy today.

3   What about tomorrow?

4   What time is good for you?

5   Can I see your holiday pictures?

6   I'm looking forward to seeing you!

B   Reading a group email

1

3   Holiday plans!

2

2   False. Erika is not free to go in July.

3   False. Sophia suggests that they go to Greece.

4   True.

5   False. Mei thinks it's a great idea to go to Greece.

3

1   a   Is August good for you?

    b   Can you do September?

2   a   I can do August.

    b   First week of September is good for me!

3   a   July is no good for me.

    b   I can't do August.

4

2   I'm visiting / going to visit Rome next week.

3   We're staying / going to stay with friends in France over Christmas.

4   He's going / going to go to Greece this September.

5   My friends are meeting / are going to meet me in town.

Unit 4 Understanding opinions

A Using Twitter

1

1 Tweets
2 follow
3 followers
4 Tweet
5 Retweet

2

1 Leah Potts's new film [✓]
2 Martin James's new book [✗]
3 The President of the USA [✓]
4 Last night's football match between Manchester Utd and Juventus. [✗]
5 The Beatbops on Talent Showcase [✓]
6 A new book [✓]

3

1 fact
2 fact
3 fact and opinion
4 opinion
5 opinion
6 fact
7 opinion
8 opinion
9 fact
10 fact and opinion

4

Positive phrases (things I like)

she's a great ...
I adore her ...
... was good, though.
I really like ...
... were amazing.
... is very good.
We really enjoyed ...

Negative phrases (things I don't like)

I hate the ...
... were awful.
I can't stand ...
She's a bad ...
... is terrible!

B Reading opinions in blogs

1

| 1 | e | 3 | b | 5 | d |
| 2 | a | 4 | c | | |

2

2 Boring grammar or interesting fiction – you choose!

3

| 1 | ✓ | 3 | ✗ | 5 | ✓ |
| 2 | ✗ | 4 | ✓ | | |

Unit 5 Registering at a language school

A Reading a language school website

1

1 Yes, it is. The school offers the course you want. Yes, the school offers the course you want. It is worth reading further.

2

1 Yes
2 Yes
3 No
4 No
5 Yes
6 Yes

B Understanding a registration form

1

1 b
2 d
3 a
4 c

2

2 27/06/1993
3 With a host family
4 Upper-intermediate
5 4 years 3 months

3

Answers will vary. See Text B for model answer.

C Reading a noticeboard

1

1 ✗
2 ✓
3 ✗
4 ✓

5 ✗
6 ✓

2

2 False
3 True
4 False
5 False
6 True

Unit 6   Arriving at a hotel

A Reading about a hotel

1

1 Room service ✓
2 A safe in your room ✓
3 Film rental ✗
4 Free Internet access ✓
5 Jacuzzi ✗
6 Swimming pool ✓

2

1 access
2 fully equipped
3 facilities
4 available
5 reception

3

1 can
2 can
3 can't
4 is
5 isn't
6 can

B Understanding notices

1

1 b   3 f   5 d
2 e   4 a   6 c

2

1 b   2 a

3

2 Leave the building immediately.
3 The assembly point on Oxford Street.
4 No, do not stop to get your bags.
5 No, do not re-enter the building.

C Reading the weather forecast

1

Thursday

2

2 False
3 True
4 True
5 False

Unit 7   Sightseeing

A Planning your trip

1

1 tour   4 views
2 performance   5 landmark
3 exhibit

2

3 Top five free places to visit in NYC

3

2 6am
3 1911
4 Manhattan and Brooklyn
5 26 million
6 Park Ave at 42nd St B4

4

1 New York Public Library

2 Central Park

3 Central Park, Times Square, Grand Central Station

4 Grand Central Station

5 Brooklyn Bridge, Times Square

6 Brooklyn Bridge, Grand Central Station

5

Answers will vary. See Exercise 4 for model answers.

B Visiting a museum

1

1 b

2 e

3 d

4 a

5 c

2

1 No

2 Yes

3 No

4 Yes

3

1 10am

2 4.15pm

3 $18

4 free

5 twelve

Unit 8   Going shopping

A Reading signs in shop windows

1

1 chemist

2 bakery

3 butcher

4 department store

5 supermarket

6 gift shop

2

1 stock

2 price

3 allowed

4 sale

5 reduction

3

1 b

2 a

3 a

4 a

5 b

6 a

B Buying something in a shop

1

1 b   4 c

2 e   5 d

3 a

2

2 Yes, you can, if you return it within 14 days with the receipt.

3 No, it won't. You must return it within 14 days.

4 Yes, you need it if you want an exchange or refund.

5 No, you can't.

3

The bath oil costs £2.99, not £3.99.

4

1 Gifts 4 U

2 Drew

3 16 March / 11:14

4 30 March

5 A free newsletter

Unit 9   Eating out

A   Deciding where to eat

1–2

1	b	3	a
2	d	4	c

3

2   San Fran Diner
3   San Fran Diner / Golden Gate Noodle Bar
4   Taj Mahal Curry House / Bella Vista Pizzeria
5   Bella Vista Pizzeria
6   San Fran Diner

4

Good	delicious	yummy	excellent
Bad	terrible	disgusting	disappointing

B   Reading a menu

1

1   burger
2   lettuce
3   fries
4   tomato
5   steak
6   ice-cream

7   cheese
8   garlic

2

(The) San Fran Diner

3

2   False. It costs $8.95.
3   False. You can also order fries, garlic bread or onion rings.
4   True
5   False. It comes in two sizes: regular or large.
6   True

4

1   San José omelette
2   shrimp cocktail / tuna salad
3   chicken wings / steak sandwich
4   Answers will vary.

5

1   b
2   a
3   d
4   c

Unit 10   Going to the cinema

A   Choosing a film

1

1	b	2	a

2

2   A Royal Affair
3   Mads Mikkelsen
4   2093
5   Somewhere in space
6   Michael Fassbender

3

excellent, superb, 'A long, slow pleasure', terrific, 'steals the show' (and the four-star ratings of both films).

4

(Sample answer)

I'd like to see A Royal Affair because I like dramas.

5

1   director
2   actor
3   cast

B   Checking film times online

1

3

2

1   Three times
2   10:00 / 20:20
3   No
4   Yes / 10:00

C Buying your ticket online

1

1   total
2   purchase
3   reserved
4   confirm
5   quantity
6   booking fee

2

The date is wrong – it should be Saturday, 11 November

The number of tickets is wrong – it should only be two (N.B. for this reason, the subtotal and total are also wrong).

Unit 11   Getting medical help

A Going to the doctor

1

1   c
2   d
3   e
4   b
5   a

2

A   Our team
B   Opening hours
C   Appointments
D   New patients

3

1   Yes
2   Call the surgery before 8.30 a.m. to get a same-day appointment

4

2   Sister Kathy Steer
3   No, the surgery is closed on Thursday afternoons.
4   12.30

5   People who can't get to the surgery.
6   Complete a health questionnaire / make an appointment for a health check.

B Going to the pharmacy

1

1   a
2   a
3   b
4   b
5   b
6   a

2

Read the leaflet inside very carefully.

3

2   True
3   False
4   True
5   False
6   False

Unit 12   Flying

A Checking in

1

1   Check-in Desk 14A
2   €10

2

1   b
2   d
3   e

4   a
5   c

3

2   €50.
3   No, you are only allowed one piece of hand luggage.
4   Yes, that's right.
5   No, you can't. You must pack sharp objects in your checked-in bags.
6   Yes, you can.

B Going through security

1

a 2

b 4

c 1

d 3

2

3 It is about what to do at security – it's very important so I will read it again carefully.

3

2 False. I must take off my shoes and put them on the conveyor belt before I go through the metal detector.

3 False. I must empty my pockets, put the things in a tray and put the tray on the conveyor belt.

4 True

5 False. I can only take liquids in containers measuring up to 100ml in a clear plastic bag.

6 True

C Boarding the plane

1

1 CAF923

2 Gate 19

3 09.55

4 37C

Unit 13 Catching a train

A Checking train information online

1

1 b

2 c

3 d

4 e

5 a

2

1 £6.00

2 09.46 / 12.01

3 London Euston / Birmingham New Street

4 No

5 The 10.03 train only takes 1 hour 24 minutes / It costs £20.00.

B Understanding notices at a station

1

1 Yes

2 Yes

2

1 False

2 False

3 True

4 True

5 False

C Understanding signs on trains

1

1 b   3 b

2 a   4 b

2

1 luggage

2 unattended

3 WC

4 alternative

5 out of order

6 alarm

Unit 14 Taking a bus

A Finding out about the next bus

1

1 cancelled   3 delayed / due

2 on time

2

1 14   2 are some   3 aren't any

3

2 It's due in 4 minutes.

3 You need the M7.

4 It's because of emergency roadworks in Granville.

5 Yes, it is.

B Understanding notices at the bus stop

1

1 b   3 a   5 a
2 a   4 b

2

1 Ticket prices

3

2 False. The only ticket prices that have changed are peak-rate fares.
3 True
4 True
5 False. They will have to pay $2.70
6 False. They will have to pay $3 because you need ID to get a concession.

4

1 in
2 for
3 on
4 on
5 to

C Reading signs on the bus

1

1 b
2 d
3 a
4 c

Unit 15 Travelling by car

A Following directions

1

b 26 minutes

2

1 b
2 a
3 d
4 c

3

2 Yes, you do.
3 Yes, you do.
4 No, you don't. You need to take exit 48A.
5 No, you don't. You need to take the first left.

B Understanding road signs

1

1 priority
2 resident
3 detour
4 required

2

1 b   2 a   3 a

3

1 b   5 b
2 a   6 b
3 a   7 b
4 a

Unit 16 Travelling on foot

A Using an app

1

1 c
2 a
3 e
4 b
5 d

2

2

3

1 4.75km
2 58 minutes and 38 seconds
3 4.6kph
4 4.8kph
5 314

B Understanding signs and notices

1

1 pedestrian
2 private
3 accompanied by
4 Hazard
5 access
6 beware of

2

1 1, 3
2 2, 4
3 5, 6

3

1 a
2 b

3 a
4 b
5 b
6 a

4

2

5

2 True
3 False
4 False
5 True
6 False

Unit 17 Newspapers

A Reading headlines

1

b The US President will visit China.

2

a 14 people were killed by a bomb.

3

b There's been a big change in education in Africa.

B Reading newspaper articles

1

E-reader revolution for Africa

2

1 c   3 b
2 d   4 a

3

1 built-in Internet connection
2 developing countries
3 digitally publish
4 non-profit organization

4

2 The program gives children in Africa e-readers instead of traditional books to help improve their reading.

5

2 False. The Worldreader program has been running for 2 years.
3 True
4 False. In their first test, they found that students who got e-readers improved their reading on tests from about 13% to 16%.
5 False. Este Nabwire thinks that African children prefer reading stories written by African authors to those written for American children.
6 True

6

Answers will vary but may include:

1 Students who got e-readers improved their reading.
2 E-readers are light and hard-wearing.
3 They can last weeks on a single charge.
4 They have built-in Internet connections.
5 It's easy to publish the work of local authors digitally on e-readers.
6 There's a very large library available to encourage children who love reading.

7

1 a   4 a
2 b   5 b
3 a

Unit 18   Magazines

A   Reading headlines and straplines

1

1   c   An interview that Jason Cowley did with Messi
2   c   Cowley is 'up close' to Messi because he interviewed him face-to-face.
3   b   Messi

B   Reading magazine articles

1

a   4   c   2   e   3
b   1   d   5

2

1   a
2   a
3   a
4   b
5   a

3

2   He says it's a game and he plays it because it's fun.
3   £32 million
4   Antonella Roccuzzo
5   Santa Fe, Argentina
6   13 years old

4

1   c
2   a
3   b

5

1   c
2   a
3   b

Unit 19   Music and TV

A   Finding out about new music

1

b   This is a website providing news about the music industry.

2

2   Good Grace
3   Griffen
4   Click here to find out more
5   Videos
6   Fargo Festival

3

1   b   3   c   5   d
2   e   4   a

4

1   in a flash
2   up for grabs
3   for good
4   on the cards
5   out of the question

B   Choosing what to watch on TV

1

1   cookery programmes   4   nature documentaries
2   comedy   5   DIY programmes
3   reality TV

2

America's Got Talent

3

1   *Batman Begins, Shrek, Gladiator* or *The Incredible Hulk*
2   *Live Athletics* and *Tour de France Cycle Race Highlights*
3   Programme: *DIY SOS* / Channel: BBC1 / Time: 8pm
4   Channel: ITV3 / Time: 8pm
5   Programme: *Legends: Roy Orbison in England* / Channel: BBC4 / Time: 8pm
6   *Big Brother*

4

Answers will vary.

Unit 20   Following instructions

A   Following step-by-step instructions

1

b   How to take photographs on the camera.

2

1	f	3	e	5	a
2	d	4	b	6	c

3

2   False. When taking a photograph, you must be careful not to cover the flash with your fingers.

3   False. When you are happy with the photograph in the view finder, you should press the shutter button halfway down to focus on the subject of the photograph.

4   True

5   False. If you want to see the photograph after you have taken it, you should press the playback button.

4

Clockwise from top left

On/off button: Step 1

Flash button: Step 2

Shutter button: Steps 4 and 5

Zoom button: Step 3

Playback button: Step 6

View finder: Step 2

B   Troubleshooting

1

Fixing problems

2

a   3 I can't switch my camera on.

b   1 I can't take a picture with my camera.

c   2 The viewfinder has gone blank.

3

1   enable

2   lock

3   charge

4   install

4

1   b

2   b

3   b

4   a

ACKNOWLEDGEMENTS

The publisher and author wish to thank the following rights holders for the use of copyright material:

Unit 1 websites
Josef Essberger for permission to use text from www.englishclub.com
Jonny Quirk on behalf of CitySocialising.com

Unit 4 Twitter images, design and content
Twitter, Inc. for the use of the Twitter logo and text from www.twitter.com

Unit 10 Film reviews
NI Syndication for two adapted articles by Kate Muir from The Times, Saturday June 16 2012

Unit 12 airport security guidelines
Bristol Airport for the use of material from http://www.bristolairport.co.uk/at-the-airport/securityguidelines/liquid-guidelines.aspx

Unit 13 website
National Rail enquiries for a page from www.nationalrail.co.uk

Unit 17 news article
Dow Jones for the adapted article e-reader *revolution for Africa* by Geoffrey Fowler and Nicholas Bariyo (http://online.wsj.com/article/SB10001424052702303768104577462683090312766.html)

Unit 18 interview
NI Syndication and Jason Cowley for an adapted interview of Lionel Messi. Interview by Jason Cowley from The Times Magazine, Saturday, June 23 2012.

If any copyright holders have been omitted, please contact the publishers who will make the necessary arrangements at the first opportunity.